PRAISE FOR **HOW TO SOUL**

In an age of relentless technological distractions, How to Soul tackles the timeless yet urgent challenge of finding meaning in our lives. With clear, engaging prose and real-life vignettes, Atara Weisberger and Rabbi Dov Lipman make a compelling case for reconnecting with the soul—the inner self that defines and animates who we are.

Peter Himmelman
Grammy & Emmy nominee, award-winning author of *Suspended By No String* & *Let Me Out*

This book is an important book; it is a book that can change your life for the better. We spend our lives running, searching for happiness, yet often miss the path right within us. Atara Weisberger and Rabbi Dov Lipman have written a powerful guide to achieving inner happiness and peace, helping us become who we were meant to be.

Rabbi Yitzchak A. Breitowitz
Rav, Kehillas Ohr Somayach

How to Soul is an inspiring guide for anyone yearning to connect with the deepest part of themselves—their soul—and come alive through that connection. In a world burdened by mental health challenges and external pressures, this book offers a heartfelt invitation to rediscover the comfort, strength, and boundless love that reside within us.

Leon VanderPol
Founder, Center for Transformational Coaching & Author, *A Shift in Being*

How to Soul is a practical guide to helping us look inside ourselves and discover who we really are. By combining real-life experiences, historical context, and powerful reflection questions, this book takes readers on a journey of self-discovery that is both healing and empowering.

Brock Mealer
Author, *Beyond 1% - Unleashing Your Potential Against All Odds*

I want to be able to take How to Soul with me wherever I go—it will be my "notebook" to revisit time and time again as needed. The anecdotes are relatable, the exercises are easy yet deeply enlightening, and the honesty throughout the book makes it truly impactful. In a world filled with uncertainty, this book serves as a guide back to our inner light, to a steady foundation, and to a renewed connection with ourselves and each other.

Nancy Spielberg
Producer, Playmount Productions

[A] guide to exploring, knowing, and growing the soul. How to Soul offers direction and inspiration for all those seeking their inner spirit.

Dr. Michael Oren
New York Times Bestselling Author & Former Israeli Ambassador to the USA

In How to Soul, Rabbi Dov Lipman and Atara Weisberger draw from ancient biblical texts and modern sources to call readers to live intentional lives of spiritual seeking. The authors speak from personal experience to help us find meaning in even the small moments of life. Whatever your faith tradition, you will find insights here to encourage your journey.

Bishop Robert Stearns
Founder and Director, Eagles' Wings

How to Soul masterfully bridges the gap between the physical and the spiritual, offering profound insights into the transformative power of the soul in achieving real healing. With deep wisdom and powerful exercises, Atara and Dov empower readers to embark on a path of healing that nurtures mind, body, and spirit. A must-read for anyone seeking to transform their life from the inside out.

Dr. Jenn Simmons
Surgical Oncologist, Integrative Oncologist, Bestselling Author & Host of *Keeping Abreast with Dr. Jenn*

Atara and Dov offer us a perspective rooted in the richness of Jewish tradition while providing wisdom that is universal and accessible to all. Their simple yet profound stories, coupled with practical exercises, make this book a valuable tool for anyone seeking a deeper connection to spirituality and self-discovery.

Rev. Madelana Ferrara
Master Somatic Therapist, Yoga Therapist & Co-author of *Beatitudes, Christ and the Practice of Yoga*

A practical roadmap that leads you... to you! The ultimate you. Well done!

Lori Palatnik
Author and Founding Director of Momentum

HOW
— TO —
SOUL

ATARA WEISBERGER
AND
RABBI DOV LIPMAN

How to Soul
By Atara Weisberger and Rabbi Dov Lipman

Copyright © 2025 Atara Weisberger and Rabbi Dov Lipman
All rights reserved.

No part of this book may be reproduced, distributed, or transmitted in any form or by any means, including photocopying, recording, or other electronic or mechanical methods, without the prior written permission of the authors and publisher, except in the case of brief quotations used in reviews or critical articles.

For permission requests, please contact the authors at:

Special quantity discounts are available for bulk purchase for fund-raising or educational purposes. Special books or book execerpts also can be created to fit specific needs. For details, write to info@BeverlyHousePress.com.

Published by

Beverly House Press
304 E. Pine St. #1058
Lakeland, FL 33801
www.BeverlyHousePress.com

ISBN: 978-1-957466-14-9
Second Edition

This book is a work of nonfiction. Every effort has been made to ensure the accuracy of the information presented. The authors and publisher disclaim any liability for errors or omissions.

Printed in USA

CONTENTS

7	Introduction
13	Chapter One: The Dawning Of The Age Of The Soul
23	Chapter Two: Finding Inner Harmony
33	Chapter Three: Stepping Into Your Greatness
49	Chapter Four: The Power Of Presence
65	Chapter Five: How We Make Decisions
85	Introduction To Chapters 6-9
89	Chapter Six: Nature And Soul
99	Chapter Seven: Music And Soul
111	Chapter Eight: Movement And Soul
123	Chapter Nine: Food And Soul
139	Chapter Ten: Your Children And Soul
155	Return Again

159	Appendix A: Additional Guidance Regarding Finding The Courage To Make Significant Decisions
161	Appendix B: Modern Day Nature-Relate Therapies
163	Appendix C: Additional Information And Data About The Connection Between Physical Activity And Mental/Physical Health
171	Appendix D: The Importance Of Raising Children With Healthy Dietary And Physical Activity Habits
173	Appendix E: Correlation Between Loving Parents And Their Children's Physical Health
175	Endnotes
187	Acknowledgements
189	About the Authors

INTRODUCTION

DEION'S STORY

He had it all by the time he was 30-years-old.

By his third decade of life, he was already a two-time Super Bowl champion with the Dallas Cowboys, played in a World Series, was a multi-millionaire, and was internationally recognized, idolized wherever he went. He was such a star that his nickname was "Prime Time."

Yet despite seemingly having it all, Deion Sanders drove his car off a cliff in an attempt to kill himself.

How can that be? How can someone who has everything so many of us strive for - success, wealth, and fame - be depressed to the point of suicide.

Deion explained: *"I was going through the trials and tribulations of life. I was pretty much running on fumes. I was empty, no peace, no joy. Losing hope with the progression of everything."*[1]

Why was he empty? His life seemed so full?

Deion answers: *"You have 100 suits but it cannot cover up your pain. You have 300, 400, 500 pairs of shoes but you cannot take a step in the right direction. You have 9 or 10 cars in the driveway but you aren't going anywhere. You have a 15,000 square foot house but you don't have a home."*

"Prime Time" survived the suicide attempt. He relates that at that very dark moment he realized that *"football and the prime time thing was what I did but not who I was."* It was at that moment that everything he believed about his value and who he was went up in smoke. It was that moment that he discovered spirituality.

In this new reality Deion recognized that he didn't really "have all that fortune." On the contrary. "They had me," he explains. *"Now it's all about trying to make the right choices."* As a simple example, he says that he can afford to drive a Rolls Royce but he chooses to drive a pick up truck. It's about what feels right to him, not what people will think of the car he drives.

In a letter Deion wrote to his 7-year-old self, he says, *"We all have a Jekyll and Hyde ..We put one out into the world to meet people before we let them see the other — who we really are. People will see Prime Time, and they'll believe that they're seeing the real Deion....But then, when you show them Deion, they won't care to see it...So it will be easy for you to be Prime Time, all the time.... Don't catch yourself trick-or-treating to the people you love....Or worse, trying to fool yourself."*[2]

Deion relates that he used to place his trust in other people, places, and things. He was always let down. Now he lives with trust in himself and God. *"I have learned to accept all things. All my days are good. All my days are learning,"* he concludes. For Deion there is no longer success or failure. Acceptance or rejection. Winning or losing. There is only learning from every situation that life throws at him. In every moment, Deion leans in instead of looking out for what those lessons are.

FROM DEION TO THE STATE OF OUR WORLD

Deion's story has resonance for so many people today.

As we look at the world around us, we see a world in distress.

We are suffering from mental health struggles of historic proportions. We see it in the statistics and we see it on the news. And demand for mental health services is outstripping the supply.

We are challenged with ideological and political disagreements that are ruining friendships, careers and tearing families apart. What does that say about how we see ourselves and others and what we value in a human being? Are we narrowing our estimation of a person's worth to their political ideology? Or do we see ourselves and others as parts of a connected whole?

Instead of feeling supported and connected, we live in a society struggling with feelings of loneliness, emptiness, constant anxiety, and an inability to be patient, understanding, kind, and giving to others. Underlying these dynamics is a lack of understanding of who we truly are and the unique value and purpose that each of us has. When we connect with our truest selves, we can apprehend and appreciate the uniqueness of others without judging or creating artificial lines of separation. We don't need to draw those lines because we understand that human value isn't a competition or a zero sum game. We can live peacefully in our own inner "house" and create space for others to do the same.

Ironically, instantaneous global communication has not been a facilitator for real connection. Quantity does not trump quality in this case. Endless posts, tweets, reels and messaging has shifted our focus away from our inner experience and that of others to a much more external and material focus. We see and project curated versions of our lives so that we no longer know with which version of ourselves or others we are interfacing. That is a painful place to be.

A PATHWAY TO HEALING

But it doesn't have to be this way.

Each and everyone of us is equipped with the solution.

It's inside of you. It *is* you.

It's the part of you that isn't your physical body.

> *It's the source of your ability to learn lessons, to mature emotionally, and to grow into a better person*
> *It's your soul.*

If that sounds lofty and distant or ethereal and inaccessible, this book will bring it down to Earth. In the coming chapters, you will get to know your soul. You will be able to hear what it has to tell you. And you will be able to lean into it as a guiding light. The book will help you find clarity and peace. And it will transform your relationships as you learn to relate to others as they truly are - as souls of infinite depth rather than bodies or what you see on the surface.

What is preventing us from identifying and connecting to our souls? Given the critical role that it plays in living a meaningful and peaceful life, why aren't we all living from our spiritual wellspring all the time?

This book will address many answers to that question: upbringing, life experiences, belief structure, high social valuation of material existence, cultural norms, awareness level, and daily habits.

There is also the toxic allure of social media that conditions us to focus outward to establish identity instead of focusing inward - to judge ourselves by everyone else's yardstick. We confuse popularity with meaning and happiness, which is a dangerous game.

Some of these factors we cannot control. This book will delve into the ones that we *can* control in order to build a strong base of soul-awareness and life purpose. The chapters are designed as a roadmap to become, as King David writes in Psalms, "like a tree deeply rooted alongside brooks of water, that yields its fruit in its season and whose leaf never withers."[3] No matter what storms come your way, you will be firmly planted in your own rich earth.

SPIRITUALITY AND RELIGION

We do not conflate religion and soul in the book. While it's true that belief in a higher power is inherent in any discussion of our spiritual selves, this book isn't about religion. And while our soul journeys can lead to religious belief, there are many ways to create a spiritual life.

That being said, we do lean into the deep well of wisdom available in ancient biblical sources. We tend to throw the baby out with the bathwater on this one. In the shadow of discomfort with organized religion, we may disregard faith-based spiritual teachings entirely.

Regardless of your spiritual starting point or religious beliefs, the sources in this book will help you connect with your soul on a deeper level.

YOUR JOURNEY

We now invite you to take this journey - to travel to the warmth, security and love that lives inside you. To the part of you that is your legacy in this life and beyond.

It is the place of pure goodness that cannot be diminished. It is your essence. Your powerhouse. And what makes you truly unique.

Throughout the book we fuse modern science with classical philosophical and spiritual sources to create a holistic picture of the workings of our inner world. We will weave the world of being - accepting, being present, holding space and honoring boundaries - and the world of doing - where we translate our inner knowing into action that can be seen and felt within and without.

Each chapter includes an exercise or meditation to help you incorporate the chapter's teaching and ideas into your daily routine. And of course, practice makes great habits. Additional meditations and resources are available on the website and in the appendix. resources.

Words that leave the heart enter the heart. This book was written from a place of love, authenticity and respect for the preciousness of each soul. We hope and pray that from this humble place, you will be inspired to seek and connect with your own inner light and source of love and truly make it your home.

HOW TO SOUL

CHAPTER ONE

THE DAWNING OF THE AGE OF THE SOUL

LIFE IS LIKE JENGA

In the game of Jenga, a tower is constructed of 54 blocks. Turn by turn, a player selects a block from somewhere in the structure and removes it. The goal is to strategically select the next block without toppling the tower. At some point, however, the structure becomes so fragile that regardless of which block you choose, the tower will collapse.

As human beings, we are not so different. Like the tower, we are made up of a set of blocks that rest upon one another to make us whole: our intellect, emotions, intuition, body, senses, strengths, wisdom, life experience and soul. Remove one block and you might not notice much. Your life will continue with just a small gap in your structure. But remove too many blocks, or pull one block from the wrong place at the wrong time, ignore one of the blocks that's balancing precariously and you risk collapsing the structure called you.

Every one of us has different components to our lives which can lead to minor collapses and struggles. These can be losses or failures which weaken our structures or behaviors which throw us off course. Sometimes this can be due to one wrong decision and other times it can be more general lifestyle choices. Those "minor" collapses are universal. They are a part of the human condition.

The challenge is to avoid monumental collapses or, even more importantly, to build yourself a strong enough base to keep your structure standing despite the mistakes and failures which we all make and experience.

WHAT IS THAT BASE?

That base is a kind of self-understanding. It's a connection to the deepest part of yourself - the part of you that holds the secret to your happiness and your purpose in life. The part of you that is entwined with your body but is not your body. The part of you that flourishes in the warm light of gentle awareness and is easily drowned out by the static of daily living. It is the one constant in an ever-changing universe. It is your essence, your home base, your eternal self, and your inner knowing. It is your soul.

As we will explain in chapter two, the soul is very much a stranger in this world. It is also a stranger to many of us. But it doesn't have to be this way. And, it must not be this way.

[Atara] *Growing up in a totally secular home, There was no spirituality or talk of soul in my house. Neither good nor bad. It just wasn't a thing. At the same time, I was a very deep thinking and spiritual kid. I remember at a young age, lying in bed frozen with fear, imagining what happens after we die. That there is this endless blackness of non-consciousness that goes on for eternity. It sent me into a full blown panic attack. When I asked my mom what happens when we die, her answer was of no comfort. She said she was taught that we "live on in the hearts and minds of people who knew us." So what? I'm dead! Who cares if you remember me? And what happens when those people die? So I did what any self-respecting seven year old would do in the face of sheer existential terror...I shoved the fear into a tiny corner and locked the little door in front of it. But the questions remained. Who am I really? Am I just a body? What makes me, me? Why am I here?*

According to Dr. Jill Bolte Taylor, a Harvard trained brain scientist, 99.9% of all human genetics are identical.[4] Only one tenth of one percent of our genes are different among people. Dr. Taylor uses that statistic to highlight our common humanity. And while that may be what science says, we know that people are in fact very different. So what is it that makes us different? Is it just the .1% of our gene variability? Is it simply the color of our eyes and the shape of our bodies?

Our uniqueness does not lie in our physical DNA. Rather, it lies in our spiritual DNA.

Spiritual DNA cannot be identified, measured or quantified scientifically. It can, however, be observed. It can be observed in our innate personality traits, our inherent strengths, our responses to challenges, our gifts and talents, and the life paths we choose. It can also be seen in the struggles we face. Every experience in our lives is meant to bring forth an aspect of ourselves and our souls that would not have surfaced without the struggle. Life at times might be painful but it always contains the potential for transformation and discovery. As a result, no two souls travel the same path in a lifetime.

[Dov] *I grew up in an Orthodox Jewish home. This meant attending religious school, prayers three times a day, wearing special articles of clothing such as a kippah (skullcap) on my head and tzitzit (fringes - see Numbers 15:37-41), keeping to the Kosher dietary rules, and observing the Sabbath including no turning electricity on or off for 24 hours. We, no doubt, were taught about God and that we had souls but religion was more about the do's and the don'ts and I recall my fear of God punishing me if I violated the commandments. I enjoyed the traditions and the structure but the concept of spirituality, understanding who I truly was, and connecting to that inner voice to guide me through life wasn't on my radar. I was living a "religious" life but it was devoid of self-reflection and, to a significant degree, it lacked meaning. It lacked 'soul'. Despite this, I wasn't searching for anything. As long as my hometown sports teams were playing well, life was fine. Or so I thought…*

Moshe Chaim Luzzato, an 18th century Italian philosopher, poet and mystic, noted that spiritual self-reflection is necessary in order to live a meaningful life. He emphasized that we must determine who we are and why we are here as the foundation of our life's journey.[5] **Oprah Winfrey made this point quite poignantly in a 2015 lecture at Stanford University: "There is no full life, no fulfilled, meaningful, sustainably joyful life without a connection to the spirit."**[6]

A PHYSICAL HOME FOR THE SOUL

If the idea of relating to yourself as a soul feels somewhat foreign or uncomfortable, you are in good company. Many of us, when we begin to notice something spiritual, may hear an opposing voice that tells us to dismiss the spiritual thought as being foolish and unscientific - unfit for rational people. But humans are not rational beings with occasional feelings. We are spiritual beings living a physical existence. How do we know this? Can you imagine a scenario where you are physically satiated in every way but still struggling inside? What is the part of you that's struggling? Can you imagine a scenario where you are physically uncomfortable or lacking in some way but have a sense of meaning and purpose? What is driving that? Have you ever experienced a sense of awe? A sense of expansiveness inside that defies proper description? Can it be measured scientifically? Can it be quantified in physical terms? Data and science are amazing for moving society forward in many ways. But as a lifestyle, they can leave us feeling empty and wanting.

EXERCISE #1
AWE AND SPIRITUAL AWARENESS

What is awe? Awe is a sense of vastness that puts your place in the world in perspective. The vastness can be physical - like seeing the Grand Canyon at sunset or the sun glinting off the rainbow in the mist of Niagara Falls - or psychological - like seeing an exceptionally courageous or heroic act of conscience. Awe has the potential to alter how you see yourself or how you see the world. It's that powerful. You may experience physical manifestations of awe such as goosebumps or changes in heart rate as well as emotional and spiritual manifestations such as a greater sense of wellbeing, peacefulness, and connectedness.

Awe can facilitate our spiritual awareness as it evokes spiritual qualities such as gratitude, humility, presence and a sense of a greater power in the world beyond the limitations of our physical reality. Awe is more commonly experienced in new and unfamiliar places or experiences. That being said, finding awe in the familiar is both possible and powerful as a spiritual practice.

Awe Experience

No matter where you are, the key is to be in the right frame of mind. This practice is designed to help you get there—to turn an ordinary outing into a series of awe-inspiring moments.

To get started, turn off your cell phone or, better yet, leave your cell phone at home so that you won't be drawn to check it. Cell phones (and other devices) can be distracting and draw your attention away from what's happening around you. Then, set off on your experience to a place of your choosing (location suggestions below).

During this awe exercise, try to approach what you see, hear, smell, or otherwise sense with fresh eyes, imagining that you're experiencing it for the first time. Then, follow these steps:

1. Take a deep breath in. Count to six as you inhale and seven as you exhale. Feel the air move through your nasal passages and hear the sound of your breath. Come back to this breath throughout your outing.

2. As you get going, feel the ground beneath you and the air on your skin, listen to surrounding sounds, and smell what is wafting from anything nearby.
3. Shift your awareness so that you are open to what is around you, to things that are vast, impressively complex, unexpected, or unexplainable, or that surprise and delight you.
4. Take another deep breath in. Again, count to six as you inhale and seven as you exhale
5. Let your attention be open in exploration for what inspires awe. Is it a wide landscape? The tiny patterns of light and shadow? The texture of an object? A piece of art, an appliance or a piece of furniture? Let your attention move from the vast to the small.
6. Ask yourself thought-expanding questions: What is new, unknown, or unexplored about what is around you?
7. Continue your experience and, every so often, bring your attention back to your breath. Count to six as you inhale and seven as you exhale. Notice—really notice—the many sights, sounds, smells, and other sensations that are dancing through your awareness, usually undetected

Once you get in the habit of experiences like this, you may be surprised by how often you have opportunities to feel awe—they are practically infinite.

As you move through your day, take note of the moments that bring you wonder, that give you goosebumps or make your chest feel more broad: These are your opportunities for awe. They may be in your neighborhood, in front of art, listening to music, or doing something together with other people. It can be in a state park or your backyard. It can be at the mall, museum or library. It can be by a body of water or in your driveway on a clear night when you can see the stars.

WHAT ARE WE MISSING?

There is another indicator that points us in the direction of soul: the current mental health crisis. If we go back to our Jenga game, as a global society, we have more building blocks, more tools and resources, than ever before. We have more wealth, more data, more access, more mobility, and longer lifespans than any generation in world history. We have enough food to feed the world, cures for diseases, and significantly fewer global citizens living in poverty.

Yet we are neither healthier nor happier. In fact, we are more anxious, more depressed and more narcissistic than at any time in history. We struggle to make sense of who we are, why we are here, and where we fit in the bigger picture. We seek answers to life's tough questions [a good thing] and definition or confirmation of our self worth from outside of ourselves [not a good thing]. We try to fill the missing blocks in our tower with pieces that don't fit. What are we missing? The pain we see around us is our spiritual selves trying to get our attention. That quiet voice that nudges but never shouts. It tugs at us gently, steadily. But the world is so noisy and confusing, alongside a contemporary misconception linking soul work to religious fanaticism, that we can't make space to hear and connect with the soul.

IF I AM ONLY FOR MYSELF, THEN WHAT AM I?

There is one final critical piece of our "Jenga game."

As a Talmudic Sage named Hillel wrote 2,000 years ago in Ethics of our Fathers, "If I am not for myself, who will be for me? If I am only for myself, then what am I? If not now, when?"[7]

Hillel is touching on a seeming conundrum. The soul is at once unique and collective. We do not live in a vacuum. We live in a world where our actions - or inaction - impact our lives and the world around us. We cannot live as if that is not the case. There is a deep invisible thread that connects us all - our common humanity - and we do not live outside of that. In fact, true happiness is rooted in living a life of higher purpose and contributing to the greater good.

But we cannot possibly impact the world around us if we do not first get in touch with our true selves and genuinely love and accept ourselves. The great Talmudic sage Rabbi Akiva taught that the well known verse "Love thy neighbor as you love yourself." [Leviticus 19:18], is "a great rule" with which to live your life.[8] Rabbi Yaakov Weinberg who headed the Ner Israel Rabbinical College in Baltimore, MD, explains: "This means that if you do not like yourself, you are not going to like anyone else. The love, respect, care, and warmth that you have for others must derive from the love, care, and respect that you have for yourself."[9]

Going one step further, according to 20th century personal development leader Rabbi Shlomo Wolbe, we cannot even begin to reach our potential as human beings unless we understand our innate value as souls. Self-improvement and healing require us to look at our negative traits and work on them.[10] So if we don't have an apprehension of our abundance of positive traits and inherent value, we can get depressed when we try to tackle our challenges.

THE UNIQUE TIME PERIOD IN WHICH WE LIVE

If this all feels like a big ask, take a deep breath. The universe is poised to help you.

There are a number of indications that we are entering a time of tremendous potential for individual and societal growth.

On December 21, 2020, a rare alignment between Jupiter and Saturn, also known as a Great Conjunction, occurred. The two planets regularly appear to pass each other in the solar system, but on this date, for the first time in 800 years, they aligned precisely at night - at 0 degrees Aquarius, enabling the world to see their "conjunction." Astrological sources say this occurrence signifies a completely new beginning. The cosmic shift into Aquarius is also a period about learning and growth around how we as individuals contribute to and affect the world around us, for good and for bad. It is a time of potential shifting from "me" to "we" and for understanding and internalizing our dependence on and connection to one another.

Ancient sources like the Talmud and Zohar teach that the world has entered its most enlightened period and will reach a near-utopian state over the course of the next 200 years. This will be a time when we overcome illness and personal physical struggles (Isaiah 35:5-6), world peace will be achieved (Isaiah 2:4), and the world will be filled with Infinite wisdom (Isaiah 11:9). Interestingly, these same sources say that leading up to this time there will be an inversion of many societal structures, including a general lack of regard for parents, the elderly, religion, and morality.

During this time, many will feel like the ground beneath them is no longer steady. The systems and structures we've looked to for security - economic, social, environmental, political - no longer feel like reliable sources of guidance. So where are we supposed to look for answers?

We would argue that we are entering a time of spiritual enlightenment, that the universe is pushing us to shed our dependence on external structures and to look inward, to our souls, for guidance. Whether you subscribe to this notion or not, it is undeniable that change is afoot. So how do we maintain our equilibrium as the universe shifts around us?

Our journey begins where all true transformation begins, your inner kingdom, self-awareness, your soul.

HOW TO SOUL

CHAPTER TWO

FINDING INNER HARMONY

[Atara] In 1996, life was pretty good. I was a year post-graduate school, working in my chosen field as an environmental educator in Washington, D.C., and living in a sweet little house in Arlington, VA with my Colombian-American boyfriend. We worked hard, played hard and explored. At the same time, I was aware of a growing sense that something was missing for me, though I couldn't quite put my finger on it. Maybe it was a depth of connection, a stronger sense of belonging, a more robust sense of purpose. Then a series of events happened that made me truly question if I was in the right place for myself. One of them was being caught in the crossfire of a drive-by shooting in the public housing neighborhood where we were building community gardens. Fortunately no one, including the 20 kids outside with me, was injured. I didn't believe in God but I certainly believed in karma. And I was under the distinct impression that the universe wanted me somewhere else. So by the time my friend from high school called to offer me a spot on a month-long touring and educational trip to Israel, I was primed. I asked him a few questions about the trip, requested a leave of absence from my job, kissed my boyfriend goodbye for a month, and got on the plane. I was curious, but my expectations weren't much beyond another life adventure. Nine months later - the happiest nine months of my life to date - I was still in Israel. It was during this time that I connected with my missing piece: my soul.

In the words of 20th century ethics author and teacher Rabbi Shlomo Wolbe, "In order to take notice of the existence of your soul, you have to totally ignore the world that you see before your eyes because the existence of the spiritual cannot be seen by the eyes. But the spiritual world is no less real than the reality of the physical *world. The soul's reality and the reality of the spiritual is no different than the reality of a table, a chair, a house or a tree. You just can't see it with your eyes. You must dig deep inside yourself to recognize the existence of your soul and the entire spiritual realm."*

WHAT IS THE VOICE OF THE SOUL?

The soul is our connection to the Divine, indeed it is a piece of the Divine. Therefore, To understand the soul's voice we must understand the nature of God's "voice." The Bible dispels the myth of God communicating with Man in a booming and thunderous voice: "Then a great and powerful wind tore the mountains apart and shattered the rocks before God, but God was not in the wind. After the wind there was an earthquake, but God was not in the earthquake. After the earthquake came a fire, but God was not in the fire. And after the fire came a gentle whisper." (Kings I 19:11-12) The same applies to the voice of the soul. It is not loud or noticeable unless we work at it and want to hear it.

It might be easiest to understand the soul in metaphor. We cannot see wind yet we feel it in the tingling of our skin when it brushes past us. We don't know where it starts and where it ends, yet we see the paths it carves in the rustling of the leaves and the movement it creates in the ripples of a pond. It can be harnessed but it cannot be trapped. It is powerful, yet it only makes a sound as it moves through other objects. The voice of the soul may feel like a yearning for meaning and understanding and the deep desire to make sense of what is happening to you. It is the part of us that is drawn to prayer, to striving, and to searching for something more in our lives. When that voice is ignored or unexplored, we may fall into a life of chasing after things the soul cannot use: glory, fame, power, money, external validation and addictions.

By the same token, when life is joyful and meaningful, when you live in line with your purpose, you may feel the expansiveness of the soul in your chest, deep in your heart. It fills you and makes you feel vibrant and alive. The soul is an integral part of your life song. When you live from it, life feels like a masterful symphony. When you live without connecting to your soul, life feels off key.

The voice of the soul also speaks through our natural talents and abilities. Maimonides teaches that relationships, memories, creativity, desires, logic, learning, and all spiritual interests all stem from the soul. He posits that after a person passes away, the spiritual, learning, and logic all continue with the soul.

> **Abraham Isaac Kook explains that "when we forget the individual soul…when we stop paying attention to the inner life of a person, everything becomes confusing and unclear…All destruction comes about only because we have forgotten and ignored the self."[11] (Shmonei Kevatzim 8:213)**

This is why the Hebrew prayer book includes the following words recited as part of the daily prayers reminding us that our essence is our soul: "My God, the soul You placed within me is pure. You created it, You fashioned it, You breathed it into me, You safeguard it within me…As long as the soul is within me I gratefully thank You."

What does the soul sound like? How can you recognize the divine flow? The universal energy?

To understand what the voice of the soul sounds like, it can be helpful to understand what it is not. It is easy to confuse the voice of the soul with its many Doppelgangers. You may think the soul is the voice of fear or reason or shame or guilt. Or the constant chatter of your conscious mind. Or the voice of doubt or control. But it is not.

So, if that is not the voice of the soul, what is?

The soul is infinite. It is expansive. It is energy and potential. It is love and connection. It is kindness and patience. It cannot be lost or destroyed. The language of the soul is consistent with those principles. You will recognize the voice of the soul as the one that gently leads you forward. It is the one that is at peace with what is and can reach beyond your supposed limitations. It is the quiet, loving and accepting voice that knows you are worthy, good and whole just as you are, while inspiring you to continue striving. It is also the voice of self-respect. The voice of the soul is never critical or judgmental, of itself or others. It does not stratify other souls as better or worse. As the Biblical verse reminds us, the voice of the soul is a "gentle whisper" and that becomes difficult to hear when life is noisy, attention-grabbing and full of commotion.

> *The voice of the soul is never critical or judgmental, of itself or others. It is a 'gentle whisper.'*

So what do you do when you want to hear what someone whispering is saying? You quietly lean in and turn your full attention to the speaker. You listen in an intentional way. If there is background noise, it can impede your ability to hear the softly spoken words. The same is true for hearing our soul. The challenge is to tune out all the noise in and around us so we can hear that eternal whisper.

A word about meditation. Life today seems to happen at warp speed. It's fast, noisy, pressured and distracted. That is not the pace or optimal environment of the soul. The soul exists in the present moment and its energy is flowing, grounded and nourishing. It isn't rushing to go somewhere or do something. It is a haven simply for 'what is' - it is the essence of being. In order to connect to the spiritual space within us, we need to slow it all down and get quiet. There isn't one right way to do that. But common to all forms of meditation is calming the mind, aligning with breath, and gaining insight.

MEDITATION #1: TURNING DOWN THE VOLUME

Our minds are busy places. And that's ok!! But in order to hear the voice of the soul, it's helpful to create a space from your constant thoughts by quieting the mental chatter. That doesn't mean the thoughts will stop. It just means you don't get taken in and consumed by those thoughts. Instead, you watch them float by like clouds.

Setting yourself up for meditation:

1. Find a location where you won't be interrupted and where you can feel comfortable sitting still for a period of time.
2. Establish a set location for your meditation sessions. Over time, your mind will associate that location with relaxation and allow you to tune in more easily to the calmness necessary to enter the realm of meditative thoughts.
3. You do not have to be in any particular position, but it is best for your fingers to be relaxed; not clasped or intertwined
4. Sit or lie down in a position that allows your muscles to relax.

Once you are sitting or lying comfortably:

*you can choose to gently close your eyes or keep your gaze soft, as if you aren't really focusing on anything in particular.

*take a deep breath all the way into your belly for a count of four,

*hold your breath gently for a count of four,

*then slowly and completely exhale out for a count of eight.

*repeat this breathing pattern three times, focusing on lengthening the out breath.

*take a few normal breaths and relax your face, neck and shoulders.

Begin to notice your thoughts.

As thoughts come to you, simply acknowledge the thought, name the feeling it creates, or express a brief word of gratitude for it when relevant. Then let the thought float away as if on the cloud, and out of your line of vision.

There is no need to judge the thoughts or judge yourself for having whatever thoughts come to you. They are simply clouds floating by - they appear, float across the mind, and gently go on their way, carried by the breeze.

Allow yourself a few minutes to notice your thoughts coming and going on the clouds.

After a few minutes, open your eyes slowly.

Take note of how your body and mind feel.

Reflection: How did allowing the thoughts to come and go without any judgment feel? How might this exercise help you hear or connect with your soul?

Fantastic job! Meditation is hard work but with practice you will master it!

The Talmud teaches that "*Just as God sees but cannot be seen, so does the soul see but cannot be seen… Just as God is pure, so is the soul pure.*" (Berachot 10a)

[Dov] *The epiphany that at the end of the day we are all souls came to me the moment my father passed away. I watched as the numbers on the machine slowly went down. Eyes closed and in a medically induced coma in his hospital bed, he was breathing and alive as the numbers dwindled. All I kept imagining was the moment he turned to me before the coma was induced and with great struggle he "punched" me in my arm and said, "thanks for being here with me kid" as well as the moments in which we both said what would be our final "I love you." The numbers hit zero and the line went flat. That was it. It was the first time I ever saw someone pass away. One moment this man who was such a life force and source of good, laughter and happiness in the world was alive. The next moment he wasn't. But his body was still lying there. Where did the person I loved and revered, with all his personality, values, and abilities go? It became crystal clear to me that my father's true being wasn't what I always saw in front of me - the community leader, judge, and handsome, put-together body with the smile that could light up a room. Rather his lifeforce and true identity was his soul. And I had no doubt that this soul - which I do often feel accompanies me throughout my life - continued onward to its next step in its journey. The recognition that my father's true identity was and is his soul, and feeling him with me on a regular basis without his physical* *presence, inspires me to recognize that my own identity is my soul. This motivates me to quiet the outside noise, tune into **my** soul and understand what I truly want in my life.*

THE SOUL'S JOURNEY

Like water cycles from the atmosphere to the Earth and back again, the soul leaves its infinite source and embarks on an Earthly journey of growth and experience. The Midrash, an ancient commentary on part of the Hebrew scriptures which is attached to the biblical text, describes the soul's journey as a spectacular story. In this Midrash, we encounter the conversation between the Infinite and the soul as the soul prepares for its transition into a physical body. The Infinite says to the soul, "There's a child waiting to be born today, you'll be its spark." So the soul turns and looks down to earth but is troubled by what it sees there: pain, struggle, confusion, and people wrongfully hurting one another. The soul pleads with God to let it remain in the safety and serenity of the spiritual world.

But then God gently 'turns' the soul so it can see a different view: people engaged in acts of kindness, meditation, prayer, and spiritual growth - and the soul is comforted. It sees that one can be a human and live with soul-awareness. The soul then says to God that it agrees to go to Earth if God promises that it can be like those soulful people. God replies, "That's not something that I can do. As you are born, the challenge becomes yours, you're on your own, it's up to you."[12]

The baby is born. A new life begins. The body and soul go through a lifetime of challenges and successes together - ups and downs, highs and lows, steps forward and steps backward. Then at its appointed time, the soul hears the familiar voice of God, this time informing the soul that it's time to travel back to the spiritual world. The soul protests: "I'm not ready to go with You. I love being here where I can grow. Let me stay here, where I am living in this body that now feels so uplifted and complete." God replies, "I've only come to take you home. Through your hard work and a life of spirit, you've earned a place right next to Me."

The imagery in the song is a powerful representation of the dichotomy of life as both a physical and spiritual being. When the soul exists in the purely spiritual realm, there is no conflict of interest. No battles to wage between body and soul. No pull towards anything other than connection to the Divine. The idea of having to leave the clarity, purity and simplicity of the spiritual world to enter a physical body, with all its opposing demands and needs, is utterly unappealing to the soul, as the song expresses. Once the soul is actually in a physical body, it forms a connection with the physical self.

THE THREE ASPECTS OF SELF

This connection between body and soul is both powerful and precious. Without the soul, human existence is transactional, coincidental. Without the body, the soul has no home - no vehicle - in this world.

This idea is expressed by 18th century mystic Shneur Zalman of Liadi, who teaches that every human being includes a fusion of two souls - the "animal soul" and the "Divine soul." The "animal soul" is what drives our desire for success in the physical world - survival, advancement and improvement. The "Divine soul" constantly seeks to connect to its Divine source. As we struggle to balance our physical drives and needs with our spiritual desires these two souls "battle" with one another. But the animal soul is not disconnected from the divine source and has the capacity to instill our interactions in the physical world with spirituality. In fact, there is tremendous beauty in the partnership of body and soul.[13] In the words of Abraham Isaac Kook, "in bringing together the body and the soul, many chambers of light and life are produced."[14]

There is one final aspect of the self: the mind. The mind is like the clearinghouse of the self. It is the seat of all your thoughts, actions, beliefs, emotions and functioning. It allows you to perceive, feel, understand, contemplate, decide, remember, move, act, and be. It is both an exporter and an importer of information, sensations and impressions. Powerful as it is, we know that the mind doesn't operate in a vacuum. Your state of mind impacts your quality of life and your choices which, in turn, impact your body and your soul.

In the words of 20th century philosopher, Aryeh Kaplan, "Neither the body, the mind nor the soul is the self. However, in another sense, the self is the combination of body, mind and soul. The three together appear to define the self."[15] The challenge is to find balance in the attention that we pay to all three aspects of our being, and to recognize the interplay between the three and how each one enhances the other.

PRETTY VEHICLE OR POWERFUL ENGINE?

Toward the beginning of Genesis, the Bible describes God instructing Abraham to leave "his land, his birthplace, and his father's home" to travel to an unknown destination. Shani Taragin, one of the foremost biblical scholars in Israel, teaches that this is not an ancient story with no relevance to our modern day lives but in actuality relates to the quest which all human beings ultimately seek. The Hebrew words God used when telling Abraham to travel were "Lech Lecha," which literally means "go to you." She explains that God is telling Abraham, and by extension all of us, to "go to yourself. Go to your essence. See who you can be. Strive for self-realization. Many of us are seeking and looking for something that is right in front of us - indeed within us. Our true selves."[16]

[Atara] I had been in Israel for all of one week. As I sat in class in the Old City of Jerusalem surrounded by thousands of years of human history and absorbing the spiritual energy around me, I could literally feel something in my chest open up and expand. There was something very powerful there though I could not yet say what it was or what I wanted to do about it. But the tug was strong. I had spent my life battling both my body and my mind. And at the same time, I had an inexpressible sense - no, really a desperate hope - that there was more to life, more to me, to humanity, to the world - than meets the eye. As the speakers' voices wove in and out of my conscious attention, I was overcome by feeling a part of myself come to life. It made me want to cry in that deeply pleasurable way. And as I looked around me, the sense of connection to myself and to the strangers around me deepened. I felt oddly at home in this ancient, foreign place, surrounded by kindred spirits, like-minded soul seekers looking for satisfying answers to life's toughest questions. I didn't know where it would lead but I needed to find out more. It was the beginning of a journey that would change the entire course of my life and beyond.

When we think of the value of our lives, we often think in terms of what we've accomplished and what will be our legacy. Those headlines are made up of countless choices in areas including how we spent our time, what we valued, and how and who or what we loved. But at the core of those choices is how we see and value ourselves. While the body and mind have critical roles to play, if we only see ourselves as physical, it is like a sleek racecar that is polished and detailed to perfection but lacking an engine. No matter how aesthetically pleasing, no matter how expensive the tires or how aerodynamic the body shape, without an engine, it won't even get out to the racetrack. It will miss the race entirely.

Our souls are the powerful engine that propels the race car forward. Without it, we are nothing more than a pretty vehicle with a lot of untapped potential.

At our core we are souls; our minds and bodies are vehicles for its expression. When we recognize all parts of ourselves, when we nurture mind, body and spirit, we experience a sense of inner harmony. That feeling of well being improves our physical and emotional resilience, breeds a sense of calm and centeredness amidst the waves of daily life, creates balance, and improves productivity. It is also the foundation for self-development and the pathway to reaching an ideal we can all achieve: stepping into our own greatness.

CHAPTER THREE

STEPPING INTO YOUR GREATNESS

[**Dov**] *"Life is beautiful."* I heard those words from the least likely of sources. My grandmother, "Bubby" as we called her ["grandma" in Yiddish], survived months of slave labor in the Auschwitz concentration camp after witnessing a Nazi official send her parents, siblings, and tens of nieces and nephews to their deaths in the gas chamber. Orphaned and alone, when Auschwitz was liberated my grandmother was sent to a displaced persons camp in Germany where she met my grandfather. They married and moved to the United States to start a new life. Despite horrific nightmares on a regular basis, having to learn a new language and culture, and significant financial struggles, Bubby raised a beautiful family.

When Bubby reached her 70's, she was on her way for a swim while on vacation in Florida, when a city bus ran a red light and ran her over. The doctors in Florida wanted to amputate her legs but an angel of a doctor in New York said he could try to save them. After nearly 30 surgeries, she was able to walk again. But she lived in constant pain, with nerve endings that created phantom pains. All the time. Excruciating pain.

This is the woman who would say "Life is beautiful." I asked her how she could say that after all that she had experienced. She responded, "I focus on all of my blessings," while pointing to a picture of her children, grandchildren, and great-grandchildren, as well as reflecting on a lifetime of giving to her community and to helping others.

To be clear, Bubby was not superhuman. Nor did she bury her head in the sand and hide from the harsh realities of life. She was very real and didn't hide from her pain. She told me that she cried. A lot. Not in front of us but in her own time and space. Whenever she was feeling the pain, she understood how to confront her suffering head on and to feel her feelings fully. But she didn't let the pain, anguish, and trauma take over her life and her overall mood. To accomplish this, she had to dig deep inside herself, confront her pain, and make the conscious decision that she was going to choose life. She loved a good laugh, volunteered her time to help elderly and lonely neighbors, enjoyed gambling for fun in Atlantic City, and prayed daily. She would say, "When I pass away, oh does God have a lot of answering to do for me." But as long as she was on this Earth - with her soul, body and mind together - she was going to get the most out of life, give as much to others as she could, and make it as enjoyable and meaningful as possible.

The spark that fueled Bubby is a reminder of the remarkable potential - the greatness - inside of every human being.

It was only after truly internalizing that we are a soul when I witnessed my father's passing that I understood how Bubby's connection to her soul, her true self, empowered her to live her life as she did.

WHAT IS GREATNESS?

Rabbi Dr. Joseph Soloveichik, a 20th century scholar and philosopher, teaches that "*Greatness in a human being cannot be suppressed or destroyed. No matter how fiendish the circumstances, however corrupt and wicked society may be, genuine holiness and greatness eventually triumphs over...opposition... Nothing can prevent the rising sun from climbing higher and higher in the sky; nobody can stop the sun from radiating heat and light. In a similar fashion, no society can stop the development and continuous growth of the tiny infant endowed with greatness.*"[17]

When you bring to mind a great person, what qualities do you attribute to them? Is it strength, wisdom, bravery, intelligence? Is it money, fame, power, influence? Are we to understand greatness as only for the lucky and the strong? That rising to high human heights is an elite opportunity? Or is greatness something everyone can achieve - a quality accessible to all regardless of circumstance or resources?

The answers of course depend on your perspective. As Einstein says, matter can neither be created nor destroyed. So if your definition of greatness is how much of the material world you possess, then the opportunities for greatness are certainly finite. The more you have, the less there is for me.

In the spiritual world, however, the pie is infinite because the Divine is infinite - beyond space and time. As the Bible relates, from that universal essence of the Creator, God 'breathed' a living soul into human beings for a specific and unique purpose. And every soul is given the exact tools, resources and challenges needed to fulfill that purpose. What is meant to be yours is available to you and I cannot take it from you. Likewise, what is meant to be mine, cannot be taken from me. In other words, competition and limited resources are not concepts born of spiritual reality. Like Deion Sanders realized after his suicide attempt in the introduction, there is no winning or losing, no better or worse, no richer or poorer in the spiritual space. There is only striving to actualize our individual potential. That's why you can have two people that put in the same effort for the same purpose (i.e. a business deal or a health issue) and have vastly different outcomes. We each have a unique path to walk. And the outcome of our efforts is custom designed for what we need to work on to become more developed souls.

That doesn't mean we don't strive for the things we want. We don't sit on the couch and wait for our blessings or challenges to come to us. But it does mean we can let go of feelings and actions that are antithetical to spirit like jealousy, spitefulness, or feelings of shame when things don't work out for us despite our best efforts.

We can take this one step further: the more I have in the spiritual realm, the more I develop myself as a spiritual being, the more capacity I have to give to others. You cannot pour water from an empty bucket. When we feel that our inner resources are depleted, no matter how much material greatness we have, we cannot give properly to ourselves, to others or to the world around us.

True greatness, at its core, resides in spiritual awareness and development and is achievable by each and every one of us regardless of - or maybe because of - the circumstances of life in which we find ourselves. It is highly individualized, and it is also directly connected to your unique purpose in life, which every single one of us has.

The Talmud (a 4th century compilation of ancient teachings and traditions) teaches that every person must believe that the world is created just for them and them alone.[18] Medieval biblical commentator Rabbi Shlomo Yitzchaki (known as "Rashi") explains this to mean that each human being is "as important as the entire world."

Rabbi Shlomo Wolbe, a 20th century spiritual mentor based in Jerusalem, elaborated on the ramifications of this teaching: "Our life story is a one time experience in the history of mankind - it never existed before and it will never be mirrored again. Each one of us must say to ourselves - I, with my unique blend of talents, skills, and strengths, born to my specific parents, born into my specific time period in my specific environment, have my own specific mission to execute. And the entire universe is waiting for me to fulfill my intended mission, because no one else in world history can accomplish my unique purpose."[19]

That unique purpose is the greatness latent inside of every human being. Everything that happens in and around us can be an opportunity to stimulate spiritual awareness and facilitate spiritual growth. How we respond to that stimulus determines whether we grow, stagnate or fall back in terms of our potential for greatness.

[Atara] *Having a spiritual practice and perspective has helped me in almost every area of my life. That doesn't mean the absolute outcome was exactly what I would have wanted it to be. But it means that the part of me that I value most - my soul and my eternal relationship with God - is the guiding light in the day to day choices I make. I don't always make the spiritual choice - my mind, body and emotions can certainly distract me. But I know what I'm aiming for even if I don't hit it every time. I know that with every decision, every situation, every challenge, I have an opportunity to strengthen my inner light, to build my eternal connection with the Divine, and to find peace wherever I am. I strive to remember that I have everything I need in any given moment to choose the highest good for myself and others. There is tremendous peace in that - knowing that the outcome is not the goal of our existence - the process is. It is choosing soul and spiritual growth through all the ups and downs of life.*

Business

For two decades I was in business for myself as a personal trainer, nutritionist, coach, and fitness studio owner. Along the way, people would often call me for advice if they were thinking about going into the field. It didn't matter if they were going to set up shop next to me or across the country, I always did whatever I could to help and mentor them. If someone asked me why I'm not worried about competition, my answer was always the same. In God's world, there is no such thing as competition. Whatever is meant for me will be mine and no one can take it away. And what is not meant to be mine, will never stay with me. That goes for every single person. There will never be a time in the spiritual universe where sincerely trying to help another person will bring anything but goodness back around to you. You can live from the place of knowing that every good deeds raises us all up spiritually.

Self-Esteem and Body Image

As a young child, I remember being a sensitive but loving and happy-go-lucky kid. I felt things deeply and had a hard time deflecting negative energy. As I got closer to my teen years, the dynamics at home became increasingly stressful for me. I often felt alone or fearful and my anxiety started to climb. By high school, that anxiety had morphed into low self-esteem and an eating disorder that would stay with me for decades.

While I would never suggest that spirituality is the answer to an eating disorder, knowing and believing that my truest self is not my body did help me through that challenge. I try to see myself through God's eyes, rather than other people's eyes, or even than through my own, because I know that I can have a skewed view of myself. I lean into what God finds beautiful: when I take care of all that he has gifted me - mind, heart, body and soul - and use those gifts for the good.

Parenting

The guiding light of my parenting style has been to create a loving and nurturing space for my children to become the people they want to be. I truly see them as unique souls with their own path, their own relationship to God, and their own journey to walk. Of course I want them to be happy and healthy and good people, but I do not have designs on who I think they should be. And indeed each of my kids are gloriously different from one another and I love that. I also worked hard to put my own ego aside to do what was right for my kids, especially in the *wake of a difficult divorce. Sometimes that meant staying quiet and channeling my pain into prayer, often times it meant choosing faith over fighting or working harder to make it all work. I don't think I could have done any of that without a strong belief in soul and God.*

IDENTIFYING YOUR UNIQUE POTENTIAL

Your well of spiritual potential is at once unique and deep. But how do you recognize it? It is reflected in your deeper qualities, gifts and abilities. It is alluded to when you feel most alive and most at peace. It also shows up in your values, resources and limitations. While self reflection can help us get in touch with and even name some of these unique soul qualities, often our spiritual potential is actualized by challenges. It is a reality of human nature that the soul rarely grows in the face of comfort and ease. Rather we grow when we are faced with resistance; resistance to how we think life "should be" and how our lives should go.

When we experience what feels like a brick wall in front of us - immovable, impenetrable, blocking our view of the other side - that is when we have the opportunity to flex our spiritual muscle. We have the choice to deflect, distract, numb out and distance ourselves from the challenge at hand. Or we can choose to grow, to stretch, to take another step towards who we can and are meant to be. Greatness is climbing the mountain of personal development - of becoming stronger, kinder, more resilient - even when it makes your legs and lungs burn with effort. The alternative is to stay safe inside the sheltering cave or descend to base camp. But you will miss the spectacular view at the top and, more importantly, a perspective on how far you've climbed as a soul and a human being.

On some level, only our Creator knows our absolute potential. That's why when life gets tough and we feel like we can't go on, we ask "Why me?" And the Creator answers, "Why not you?" That answer is not flippant. It's actually a vote of confidence. Tough times are God saying to you, "I know you. I know what you can be. I know this hurts. I also know that this can make you greater. You don't see it now, but you will if you want to. Let this challenge make you greater. Let this challenge make you better. Let this challenge make you stronger."

In the book *Radical Remission*[20], author Kelly A. Turner, PhD, writes about a 35-year-old woman, Saranne Rothberg, mother of a five-year-old girl, who was diagnosed with stage 4 breast cancer after being told for years that she had a postpartum breast infection. Inspired by Norman Cousins' story, Anatomy of an Illness, Rothberg decided to incorporate laughter, fun, joy and playfulness into her treatment plan. Even as Rothberg was suffering physically from her cancer treatments, her deep dive into comedy and laughter infused her with a sense of joy and a zest for life that inspired all those around her, including other chemotherapy patients.

Spiritual before her diagnosis, the cancer experience deepened Rothberg's soul connection and she realized that cancer was a wake up call. She told herself that despite the diagnosis, she doesn't need to die. She just needs to live: to wake up and meet the call. So she leaned into her thinking and asked herself what she was supposed to learn from cancer, what she is here to teach because of it, and how she can make the world a better place as a result. The answer that came to her became her life's mission. Rothberg founded the organization The ComedyCures Foundation to bring humor, hope and a comedic perspective to patients in the throes of cancer treatment. She incorporated a wide range of healing modalities into her treatment plan - both conventional and alternative - and continued her work helping other patients thrive in the face of cancer. More than 16 years after being diagnosed with stage 4 breast cancer, Rothberg is alive and well and a testament to the power of mind.

[Dov] *While Saranne is living and doing so much good in the face of her illness, the lesson applies even when the story doesn't have "a happy ending." My father passed away from his cancer but while in the hospital he managed to bring joy to those around him. When he died the nurses all cried because they would not hear the non-stop jokes and funny comments that my father shared with them on a daily basis. "Your dad brought so much joy to our job which usually means stress and sadness," one of them explained.*

The prophet Isaiah writes: *"For just as the rain and snow descend from heaven and will not return there, rather it waters the Earth and causes it to produce and sprout, and gives seed to the planter and food to the eater."* (55:10)

Rabbi Yehudah Aryeh Leib Alter, known as the "Sfat Emet" and the third spiritual leader of the Hassidic sect known as "Ger" (from Gola Kalwaria, Poland), understood this prophecy as a metaphor for the soul's journey and mission in this world. Just as the rain comes to the Earth with a specific goal - to water the land, enable crops to grow, and feed humanity - the soul comes to Earth with a mission and purpose to fulfill before it returns to its Source.[21]

The value of finding your soul purpose can go far beyond the benefits to your own life. Each soul has both an individual and a collective purpose. Luzatto teaches that when we work on ourselves and live up to our spiritual calling we have the capacity to impact and lift up everyone around us and even the entire world. If your purpose is left unfulfilled, it leaves a gap in our collective mission to perfect this world to the best of our ability.

That all sounds pretty important. So how do you begin to figure out what that purpose is?

Rabbi Zadok ha-Kohen Rabinowitz, a 19th century philosopher and spiritual mentor, recorded an ancient tradition that if you are consistently challenged in one specific area of life, then your purpose in this world relates to overcoming that specific challenge. Maimonides takes this in a more proactive direction and says that every one of us has one spiritual area of life which brings us the most joy and fulfillment. Working on these to the point of perfection is your ultimate mission.[22]

EXERCISE #2
SEVEN DAYS OF SOUL

This exercise is designed to get your wheels turning about your mission in life - what you are here to work on, achieve, and contribute. The exercise is divided into seven days of reflection. The first six days have question prompts to contemplate, with the sixth day's questions bringing it all together. Day seven is a sabbatical of quiet meditation and alignment. This Sabbath is a chance to feel into and integrate your self-reflections as a part of you and is the beginning of stepping into your greatness.

It is important to have a tangible record of your reflections and answers and you can use any of the formats listed in Exercise #1.

Day 1

When you were a child, what did you dream of being?

What is the most meaningful compliment someone has given you?

Day 2

What special gift do you have that you can give to the world?

When do you feel the most fulfilled?

Day 3

If you could solve one problem in the world, what would it be? What makes that important to you?

If you could solve one problem in your life, what would it be? What makes that important to you?

Day 4

If you had to take a best guess at your life's purpose, and just get started with something that excites you, what would it be?

What does your heart say you are to do with your life?

Day 5

What personal challenges have come up for you repeatedly?

What lessons can you learn from those challenges? How can you help others with those same challenges?

What is the most important thing in your life?

Day 6

How would you answer the question "Who am I?"

What do you think your soul's unique purpose is during your lifetime?

Day 7

Rest your mind. Set down your pen or turn off your computer. Tune into your heart. Listen for resonance with these reflections deep inside you. You may feel a deep sense of peace or a quiet but powerful joy in this space. You may feel a rising sense of purpose and a feeling of wholeness. Whatever you are feeling, honor it. And know you can always come back to Seven Days of Soul when you want to connect.

CHALLENGES TO SELF-AWARENESS

Even if you begin to focus on self-awareness, there is a challenge our world poses to staying in that centered place. Our focus on external approval, particularly through social media, is warping and undermining our connection to ourselves and our perception of our lives. We take ourselves out of the moment to record and post every experience. And we bend the lens of life by presenting a partial picture of what's really happening with us. Because the richest flavors of life come through the relay of information between our senses and our awareness, if you are seeing the experience through the lens of external validation, you rob yourself of the pleasure of the moment. Instead of living life, you live for 'likes'.

Like an adolescent driven by peer acceptance, the social media culture is founded on and perpetuated by our seemingly insatiable need for external approval. But unlike an adolescent who is seeking approval of those in his or her social circle, social media drives us to crave acceptance from abject strangers who are likely to never encounter us in real life.

[Dov] *I had to undergo a shock therapy of sorts to internalize that my identity is independent of what others think of me. In 2011 my life shifted course in dramatic fashion. Religious extremists moved to my neighborhood in suburban Jerusalem. Their fanaticism led them to try to pressure and even coerce their new neighbors to adhere to their rigid lifestyle. Their primary focus was on women dressing "more modestly." While I am religiously observant, I am against religious coercion. My belief in freedom of choice and different types of people co-existing with tolerance and respect for one another led me to head the community effort against these extremists. This brought me to the public eye and to eventually run and get elected to the Knesset in 2013. My focus was to improve my country. I had the best of intentions. But I wasn't prepared for the spiritual challenges that came with the change from being an unknown educator to becoming a public-figure parliamentarian. People began to write Facebook posts and opinion columns either in support or against me. I was flooded with emails either supporting or criticizing me. Talkbacks on news articles about me became a steady stream of lavish praise or harsh, at times painful, comments about my ideologies, policies, and political activity.*

It was both crushing and "elevating" and both negatively impacted my connection with myself and my own inner truth.

At times the negative brought me to a very dark and gloomy place. There were moments when it made me want to give up. Even worse, that sadness made spiritual connection nearly impossible. The opposite happened as well. Because of the very public praise that I would receive from my supporters I began to crave and seek that positivity to help build me up as a person. The headlines and Facebook likes started to determine my confidence about what I was doing and even whether I should or shouldn't continue with a certain course of action.

In short, I began to see myself solely through the lens of what others were saying about me. The spiritual disconnect that this turmoil caused was palpable. But it was easy to ignore that reality with the justification that I was doing important work. I made my needs and spiritual health less important. At times, I even convinced myself that the spiritual sacrifice was chivalrous given the positive impact my work had for my country and people.

The Knesset went on its first significant recess four months after I was elected and my parliamentary activity was paused temporarily. I suddenly felt like something was missing. The daily highs from positive media stories about me and my political party disappeared. I found myself craving them and even thinking of what I could post to be able to garner praise on social media.

That jolted me.

I took some time to think - a freedom I had as the insanity of the Knesset work hours came to a halt. For a time, I was liberated from the shackles of the cocoon within which I was working day and night. I realized that my highs and lows, and my entire identity, had become based on numbers of Facebook likes and articles in the media empowered me to dig deep and to find the strength to remind myself that others don't define who I am.

I remembered that as long as I am following my inner voice and acting from my true inner self as my guiding light (while of course seeking advice and guidance from those whom I trust and love), then it doesn't matter what others think of me. I was blessed to return to the next Knesset session driven by the values and ideologies which came from my soul, enabling me to wake up every day keeping my eye on my goal, which was to improve my country and make things better for my people. That filled my life with meaning and happiness.

Author and speaker Simon Sinek touches on a relevant topic in his book *The Infinite Game*.[23] Sinek describes the difference between an Infinite versus a Finite game in life. Finite games are ones where the rules are fixed and clear cut, there are winners and losers, and the thrill is high but fleeting. He gives sporting events, chess, and promotions as examples. By contrast, an Infinite game has no defined winners and losers, no endpoint where one can say the effort is "done," no peak thrill experience. Rather, the satisfaction in an Infinite game comes from the steady effort we put forth towards a meaningful and impactful goal, what Sinek calls the pursuit of a "Just Cause". We trade the fleeting but powerful flash of feel-good endorphins for the deeper pleasure of contributing towards the creation of a better world.

THE PERILS OF EXTERNAL VALIDATION

If we apply Sinek's language, we can see that social media is one of the greatest current challenges we face to having a healthy identity. Social media plays right into a Finite mindset. It plays on people's fears and insecurities. It feels competitive rather than abundant. It creates a false sense of security. It takes you out of reality and into a projected universe. And it sweeps the rug of self-definition and true life satisfaction out from under your feet. The negative and finite mindset that social media leaves in its wake makes it exponentially harder to appreciate what you have and to maintain a sense of presence. Only the strongest can survive that pull and remain steadfast in their presence.

NBA superstar Lebron James, a player who has been criticized often in the public sphere for his decisions, was asked what he thinks about people's statements against him. He replied that he doesn't care what people say about him because *"Our quest and our journey is not predicated on what everybody said. You are going to have five people that love you out of ten. Then you have five people that hate you out of ten. That's just the way of the land. No matter what you do. You can be a guy who literally goes to work at Starbucks, and there's going to be four or five customers that come in and hate the way you made the chai tea latte. It's just how it works. And the faster you can realize that happens, the better off you'll be, because you're not going to respond or give that too much energy."*[24]

Renowned psychiatrist and Talmudic scholar Rabbi Dr. Abraham Twerski teaches that if we let that self-awareness go, if we get caught up in the reactions and opinions of others, we end up like an eddy of water behind a rock, swirling but not really going anywhere.

"Allowing others to establish your identity runs the risk of making yourself into a chameleon, as you continually change identities according to what others say you are. At best you become a composite of the various identities you assume. It should be evident that many important decisions in life depend on your identity, and the decisions made in the presence of a vacillating or poorly defined identity may be less than optimum."

Twerski goes on to say that a genuine identity cannot be contingent on any external source. You have a bona fide identity only if you are a product of your own self-evaluation. If you are dependent on anyone else or anything else for your identity, then you do not have a true identity.

Dr. Twerski had been a successful rabbi and therapist for years when he finally had his first real vacation at the hot springs in Arkansas. He went in for his first spa treatment and after 5 minutes in the water by himself he asked the attendant to let him leave. The attendant told him that there were 25 more minutes. Twerski begged the fellow to let him leave. But then he began to analyze why he wanted to leave so badly. After all, wasn't this the moment he had waited years to get to? No telephone? No people asking to meet with him? Just some quiet time to himself? It suddenly hit him. He had been thriving off the fact that he was needed. His identity had become the congregant he was inspiring or the patient he was treating. But in the process he had lost touch with his true inner self.[25]

Alone with himself in the hot spring, he felt like he was trapped in a small room with a person he didn't like. What could be worse than that? In that moment he understood that he needed to begin the challenging and sometimes painful process of getting to know his own soul and working to create a loving relationship with that essential part of himself. The realization opened an internal door for him. When he walked through it, on the other side of the door was a happier, more meaningful life, less affected by external situations and challenges, and ready to reach toward his true potential. On the heels of this internal work, Rabbi Twerski spent the rest of his life spreading the word about the importance of soul-awareness and self-awareness as a foundation of a happy and fulfilling life. To that end, he wrote over 90 books related to this topic including *I've Gotta Get Out of My Way!*, *Like Yourself: And Others Will, Too*, and *The Problem Was Me : How to End Negative Self-talk and Take Your Life to a New Level*.

In addition, he founded the Gateway Rehabilitation Center in Pittsburgh, Pennsylvania which states as its core belief that *"recovery from addiction involves healing of all dimensions of a person—physical, intellectual, emotional, social, vocational, and spiritual. The process involves an improvement in self-awareness and self-image."*

One of the most powerful descriptors of the dance between internal and external identity is from early 19th century spiritual leader Menachem Mendel Morgenstern of Kotzk, Poland (known as "the Kotzker Rebbe") . He taught: *"If I am I, because I am I, and you are you because you are you, then I am I and you are you. But if I am I because you are you, and you are you because I am I, then I am not I and you are not you."* [26]

If we were to translate the Kotzker Rebbe's words into simpler terms, it may read something like this:

> *"I was uniquely created to be me. You are uniquely created to be you."*

If I own and embrace my true self from within myself and you do the same, then each of our unique selves can shine. If I am merely a reflection of how you see me or you are merely a reflection of how I see you, then our uniqueness is lost to ourselves and to the world.

So how do we take back the reins and create our own measuring stick for success? How do we live in confidence that it is ok to be our own best influencer? How do we value ourselves for all that we are right now and not focus on all that we lack? How do we make sure that we are living in a manner which empowers our soul-based potential to emerge?

We create presence.

HOW TO SOUL

CHAPTER FOUR

THE POWER OF PRESENCE

[Atara] *Until last year, my coaching training and approach has been largely what is called transactional coaching. It focuses on the achievement of desired goals and improved performance and is primarily about action, accountability, and performance. The other part of my training has been as a health and wellness consultant. As a consultant, the role presumes that I am the "expert" of a certain body of knowledge, namely how clients can achieve their health and wellness goals. It is a "top down" approach and supposes that I have the answers for how other people and organizations can achieve their stated wellness goals. In both cases, the success of any given session is largely dependent on my skill as a coach. Do I ask the great questions? Do I have the right answers? Can I communicate effectively so I can help the client shift? The coach is in some ways more active than the client in these sessions. As a result, changes in clients are often superficial because they are anchored in their "doing" but not in their "being."*

As my desire for personal transformation and growth got louder in the last couple of years, I started searching for a deeper healing modality for myself and my clients. I came across a book called "A Shift in Being" by Leon Vanderpol and I dove right in. A few weeks later I registered for Leon's intensive Deep Transformational Coaching course. In this course, we left the world of "doing" and embraced the world of "being." Instead of asking the 'right' questions, we learned the power of silence to create a healing space. Instead of setting goals, we became spiritual partners in the journey towards greater self-awareness. Instead of having all the answers, we listened deeply for whatever wanted to arise in a session. And instead of cheerleading for a job well done, we honored the courage to show up authentically.

As we coached one another as students, we luxuriated in the cocoon of non-judgemental space. In this warm bath of acceptance, we experienced pain as a gateway to self-understanding and personal growth rather than as a blemish. We felt into the dark spaces of our hearts and minds and found doorways to our souls there. We cried. We reflected. We felt. We released. We held each other in our hearts and connected as souls. We learned how to be present. And we witnesses and the power of presence to heal us from the inside out."

Presence means connecting to others and to yourself from a spiritual place.

Envision walking into a room and seeing many people there. If your mind tells you that everyone is looking at you and thinking about you, this will lead you to focus on yourself, your appearance, and your ego. That in turn will make you uncomfortable or proud - both feelings driven by externals. But if you center yourself in your soul when entering the room, and you are genuinely focused outwardly, you will have a completely different experience. You will notice the people around you, you will appreciate the sounds and colors in the room, and you will feel at ease and a sense of comfort because you know who you are from within. You are not concerned about what others are thinking and can totally relax and enjoy whatever the experience may bring.

LEARNING FROM MOSES

The Divine communicates with humans throughout the Bible. But the first time God ever defines himself to Man occurs at the Burning Bush. Moses asks God, when I tell the Israelites that you came to me, they will ask me what is Your Name? What should I tell them? And the Divine responds, "I am who I am." (Exodus 3:14) God defines Himself as Presence and Existence, and tells Moses to identify Him to the Israelites as simply "I am." The Bible then exhorts Man to strive to walk in God's ways (Deuteronomy 10:12). If God sees himself as Present - existing, aware, in the moment - then surely the key to understanding ourselves and the Divine power and potential waiting to explode from within ourselves rests with that "simple" formula - being present.

Moses clearly took this message to heart. For the next 40 years of his life, the Israelites tested his patience time and time again - challenging his authority, questioning his decision making, and even mocking him. All this despite the fact that he was the one who led them out of devastating servitude and persecution in Egypt. Moses managed to not only absorb the constant blows from his people but replied to their constant complaining, whining, negativity and wrongdoings by advocating for them before God! He literally saved the people who wanted to kill him (source). How was Moses able to withstand the horrifying attacks against him and his character without losing his temper and forsaking the people of Israel?

Moses' greatness was rooted in an understanding that the part of him that mattered most was not the part of him that was under attack by the people. He embraced the notion that his ego might be bruised and battered but his true and higher self - his soul - remained whole and connected. And only Moses and the Divine could access that most essential part of him.

Tied into that is Moses's great humility. *"Moses was a humble man, more humble than anyone else on the face of the earth."* (Numbers 12:3) Humility is not weakness nor is it a lack of self-esteem. Humility stems from gratitude. Humility is gratitude for the gift of spirit that is your essence and its boundless capacity for love, compassion, endurance, and connection. It comes from gratitude for the gifts you have been given as your soul entered your body at birth in the form of skills, talents, abilities, and interests which help define your spiritual mission. Moses exemplified this spiritual trait. He knew his strengths and his weaknesses. He was neither proud of his strengths nor critical of his weaknesses. He knew that all he had and all he was allowed him to fulfill his mission in life, to give and grow in ways unique to him. It was this humility that allowed him to interpret the angry accusations waged at him for what they were - fear and a cry for help - which awakened his compassion for the Israelites rather than triggering a shame or ego response within himself. His humility allowed him to stay in a place of connection with those who were fearful and crying out instead of reacting, judging or lashing out. Instead Moses stepped up, again and again, to bear their burden with them.

Said differently, true humility provides the power of total objectivity which allows for personal growth. Moses had clarity that the challenges from the Israelites did not occur in a vacuum. They were not meant to become anger-causing moments in which he lashed out to defend his image and dignity and push away any shame. Rather, Moses understood that the Israelites' admonishments were opportunities for spiritual growth, moments to connect with his Creator, and reminders of his mission and his purpose in the world was more important than what others thought of him. Moses stayed the course.

Until he didn't.

Until that one time when Moses lost his focus, wasn't present, and allowed the people to anger him. He hit the rock instead of speaking to it as God commanded him, and labeled the people as "rebellers." And the consequences were devastating. Moses was no longer capable of leading the people into the land and had to pass away beforehand, ceding the position of leader to Joshua who led the people into Israel. It wasn't a punishment. It was an acknowledgement that Moses could no longer maintain his sense of presence - his emotional equilibrium - in the face of continued resistance from those he led. It was also a recognition that Moses had accomplished his life mission and it was time for Joshua to take over.

If we use the story of Moses as a starting point for defining presence, we can conceptualize it as several levels of awareness that exist simultaneously. Cultivating these aspects of self allow you to tap into the most powerful version of you:

SELF

Stay true to your core self

Embrace faith over fear

Live fully in the moment

Free yourself from *unhealthy* egotism

STAY TRUE TO YOUR CORE SELF

Chapter Two explained the process of connecting to your core self and included an exercise to help you begin to understand your mission and purpose. The next step is to familiarize yourself with what it feels like when you are living from your core self and when you are being pulled toward forces outside of yourself. This thought exercise will help you connect with that awareness.

> **EXERCISE #3**
> **RECOGNIZING THE PUSH-PULL**
> **OF OUR INNER DIALOGUE**

I. Sit comfortably in a quiet spot where there are no distractions. Take a few slow deep, calming breaths and feel your body relax with each long exhale. Relax your neck and shoulders. Soften the muscles of your face and soften your gaze.

II. Call to mind a recent situation that required you to make a choice between acting on your inner sense of what is good and right for you or what you think someone else would want you to do.

III. Feel into the memory. What feelings come up for you when you sit with the memory What felt at stake for you in this situation?

IV. **Reflections:**
   a. Recall the dialogue in your mind - sometimes two distinct voices - as you deliberated what to do.
   b. Which voice did you honor? Which voice did you silence?
   c. What made the difference in your choice? A thought? A mantra? An emotion or feeling? A consequence?
   d. What was the impact of your decision? [Practical, emotional, spiritual, or physical].
   e. On a scale of 1-10, with 1 being almost none and 10 being complete presence, how would you rate your presence when you made the decision?

f. What would help you raise that score next time you are in a similar situation?

You can note your answers as a journal entry and you can repeat this exercise as a regular part of your self-reflections in the future.

EMBRACE FAITH OVER FEAR

The Biblical Hebrew word for "faith" is "*emunah*." Hebrew words are generally formed from root letters which enable us to comprehend the essence and deeper meaning of the words we use. The root of *"emunah"* is the Hebrew letters "aleph," "mem" and "nun," which spells out "*Amen,"* meaning "authenticity" and "truth." "Faith," therefore, does not refer to a specific religion or living based on belief in something external but, rather, following the guiding light of your true, authentic self. This is why the Hebrew word for an artist, a person who expresses their inner selves via their works, is "*Oman,*" stemming from that same exact three-letter root. And this is why it is universally accepted that prayers are followed by the word "*Amen,*" which comes from that same three-letter root. We are declaring, "let the words of the prayer become the true reality."

Throughout our lives we can be held back by any number of fears - "I am not good enough," "I am not deserving," "I am afraid of failure." The source of those fears differs from person to person but can stem from the structure of our family of origin, life experiences, cultural expectations, habitual thinking patterns, or unmet emotional needs. The problem with these negative and limiting beliefs is they prevent our inner essence from being present throughout our lives. We can take this a step further and suggest that the Creator puts us in specific environments, presenting situations and challenges to grow through and learn from. But we have a choice how we respond to those challenges. If we shame and blame ourselves and others, it moves us away from *emunah*. If we tap into our soul connection, we can see our challenges as stepping stones to a deeper connection with our true selves and, by extension, to the Divine.

MEDITATION #2
RELEASING NEGATIVITY FROM YOUR SOUL'S EARLY YEARS ON EARTH

All of us have experienced pain and hurt growing up. Some experience more acute and damaging pain than others but each according to your own soul journey. No matter where you are starting from or what you are carrying with you, your soul is the guiding light out of the darker parts of yourself. This inner light is unsullied by trauma or pain and yet carries the weight of those challenging experiences. This meditation is designed to help you begin to release any distorted or negative energy blocking the light and allow for the fullest, brightest expression of your inner essence.

Begin this meditation by finding a quiet and comfortable place to sit.

Close your eyes and take two long slow breaths in and out, focusing on a longer exhale than inhale.

While breathing comfortably, begin at the top of your head and slowly relax the muscles of your face, your shoulders, your hips and glutes, legs, and feet.

Feel your body get heavier and melting into the chair - warm, relaxed, muscles softened.

Imagine yourself as a young child. Just observe your young self for a few moments in whatever setting and situation which comes to mind immediately.

What does your hair look like? What do your eyes show? What sounds do you hear your young self make? What is your demeanor? What is around you?

Now imagine a dark cloud on one side of your child self. The cloud is foreboding, heavy, frightening. As you look closer at the cloud you see what the cloud is made of....sadness, pain, hurt, fear. Dark memories swirl inside the cloud. Flashes of lightning within the cloud illuminate the painful emotions generated by the memories.

Out of these emotions, you created stories about yourself. You are not wrong for creating these stories. You created them as protection and for survival. The stories might sound like "I'm not enough" or "It's not safe to trust" or "I am not worthy" or "I don't deserve…"

But now those stories are blocking your inner light - your soul's light.

So take a deep, cleansing breath and walk over to your young self. Kneel down and gather the child into your arms. Pure love is all you feel and pure love is what you communicate in that embrace. The love, acceptance and unconditional affection you feel for the child creates a deep sense of peace and safety and allows the child to release the dark cloud of stories back into the atmosphere. The two of you watch it diminish as it floats away.

Holding the child's hands, stand and take a step back. You now see a light, bright, soft cloud on the other side of the child. The cloud is filled with laughter, creativity, dreams and love. In the cloud are the warm, positive flashes of memory. The emotions that seep into you are joy, lightheartedness, expansiveness and possibility.

Turn your attention back to your younger self. See how your face lights up? How your smile emanates from your soul? Remember how much your young curious and exploratory self loves to play and imagine and create?

Both you and your younger self are here together. Embrace the child again and feel the child's pure love envelop you back, reminding you that you are the child and the child is you.

Repeat this meditation anytime you feel the weight of your inner pain preventing you from moving forward. It takes a few minutes of your time that can impact your life for hours, days, weeks, and more.

When we are true to our authentic selves, connecting to the soul through presence we live in faith and trust rather than turned off course by fears. We never know what the future will bring. Fear is the assumption that we do know, that it could be painful, that we won't be able to handle what may come our way. When you live from a spiritual space, from *emunah* or belief that your spirit is your source of truth and unlimited capacity - you view challenges as opportunities to become a greater human being. You understand that no human being can take away your potential or your dignity. That no circumstance is pointless or futile. You can stay present in the moment knowing that in every situation - difficult or otherwise - is an opportunity to grow, to become more of who you are meant to be.

LIVING FROM PRESENCE OR LIVING TO PLEASE?

Imagine sitting in a business meeting and your superior asks you and your co-workers to act in a manner which goes against your core inner values. You can choose to not be present by disconnecting yourself from your true inner self at the moment, remain quiet and go along with the demand. That is acting from a place of fear. Fear of what others will say about you. And even fear of losing your job. Or you can be present, connect to your inner voice and true to your inner-self, explain why you disagree and why you cannot act in accordance with the superior's wishes. That is acting out of faith.

Your child comes home from school and tells you that he or she is being bullied. Your desire to protect your child from physical danger nudges you to encourage them to lay low and give into the bullies' demands. That is acting out of fear. But bullying is wrong. You know that. And your child knows that. Furthermore, your child has done nothing to warrant bullying behavior. You know that. And your child knows that. Aside from going against your inner voice in the here and now, what are you teaching your child for the future by instructing them to avoid conflict when being bullied? That they should allow fear to overcome their authentic selves throughout their lives? What kind of lives will they lead if that is how they are raised? Guiding them to not give in to the bullies and to have the courage to work with school authorities to confront the bullies is living with authenticity. It's living with "*emunah*." It's living with faith over fear.

In both circumstances, could there be devastating consequences? Loss of job or even physical harm? Life? Yes. But when you live with the "Emunah," that comes along with presence, you recognize that you don't live in the bubble of the physical consequences of your decisions. You recognize that there is something deeper to live or even die for. And living life based on the authenticity of "Emunah," brings peace of mind and calm as opposed to the discomfort and even pain inherent in living with inner fraud and inner falsehood. That is the rewarding reality of faith over fear.

LIVE FULLY IN THE MOMENT

Woody Allen is quoted as having said that 80% of life is showing up.

We disagree.

When God instructs Moses to climb Mount Sinai to receive the Bible, He says: "Ascend to Me to the mountain and be there." (Exodus 24:12) If Moses will be atop the mountain why does God need to add "and be there?" Where else would he be? 18th century Hasidic master Menachem Mendel Morgenstern, known as the Kotzker Rabbi, answers that God is telling Moses that it's not enough to simply climb the mountain. Doing so would be lacking terribly if he wasn't truly "there" and present. The Divine Revelation at Sinai itself would have been lacking if Moses lacked presence, since only with presence would his true essence and potential be there to be impacted by the experience.

Yes, showing up is a necessary first step. But showing up alone, without living in the moment, will leave one without the benefit of fully gaining from any given experience.

Award winning actor George Clooney doesn't own a smartphone.

Speaking at a press conference in 2018, Clooney said: "I was at an event with [then American president] Barak Obama a few years ago and everyone was shaking hands with their phones filming him. They can't say they met the president, they can only say they filmed him."

Clooney had the same reaction to people attending concerts and filming them on their phones. "People are losing a little bit of their living and their life because they are just filming the concert rather than enjoying it."[27]

True presence and living with a constant connection to your inner self requires focus and living every moment fully. Not thinking about your next appointment. Not relying on a picture to capture the moment. And not immediately having to share the moment with those who aren't there.

One way to anchor yourself in the moment is to tune into your senses. Whether sitting, standing or moving, when you want to bring your awareness into the here and now, ask yourself the following:

What are five things that I see right now?

What are four things I hear right now?

What are three things that I can physically feel right now?

FREE YOURSELF FROM UNHEALTHY EGOTISM

All human beings must have an ego in order to get anything done. The first three aspects of SELF teach that you must focus on the unique gifts that you have at your core, in order to fulfill your purpose in life. However, an unhealthy ego can lead to a self-absorption that can take you off the rails as you try to pursue your life's purpose.

How does one accomplish this delicate balancing act? How does one avoid crossing the precarious line between healthy self-awareness and unhealthy self-worship?

The answer lies in the most unlikely of spaces: gratitude.

What's in a thank you?

Gratitude is an acknowledgement that we need each other. That we can't do this life alone. There is no shame in that. It is part of the human experience.

[Atara] *I recently went hiking with a friend who is a therapist. I asked her what overarching lessons she's learned working with clients from many walks of life and at all different stages. She said that she's learned that all people are seeking connection and meaning. She noted that genuine connection is harder to come by now than it has ever been and it's the root of much suffering in her clients.*

Possibly more than any other species on the planet, humans need other humans to survive. The human infant is helpless longer than any other creature before it can take care of itself. Why is that? Why are we so dependent for so long? Why do we need communities and partnerships and other people to survive and thrive?

In Hebrew, the word for love is *Ahava* which comes from the root word *'Hav'* which means 'to give'. When we give, we create a connection between ourselves and the recipient. When the recipient acknowledges that giving through gratitude, they complete an energetic circuit that builds a positive bond. When the giving occurs but the recipient does not feel or express gratitude, the bond then only travels in one direction, from giver to recipient. After a time, that bond can more easily break.

That is not to say that we give with the expectation of receiving. That is Machiavellian. Rather, if our giving is met with gratitude, it closes the circuit and strengthens the relationship bond. It builds the giver and builds the recipient. How is that so?

When we express gratitude, it means we can perceive goodness in our lives. When we perceive goodness, we feel happier and more satisfied with what we have now. In the words of the *Ethics of our Fathers*, "Who is wealthy? The person that is satisfied with what they have." Gratitude is an expression of real-time satisfaction.

The best template for the gratitude circuit is the parent-child relationship in its ideal form. In a healthy parent child relationship, the parent gives unconditionally year after year after year, not expecting the child to give back to them. Rather, an emotionally stable parent wants the child to pay it forward by raising their own children with unconditional love.[28]

So what closes that giving circuit? You got it. Gratitude.

FEELING APPRECIATION

A child who can see and express thanks for all the parent does is at once a happier person themselves for seeing the good and feeling appreciation, and the parent wants to give more when what they are already giving is appreciated.

Let's tie this back to our question about why humans are dependent longer than any other species. God delivered the Ten Commandments to Moses on two stone tablets. One tablet contained five commandments that emphasized the relationship between man and God. The second stone tablet taught commandments that emphasized the relationship between people. The commandment to honor one's parents is the fifth commandment on the first stone tablet, the one emphasizing the Man-God relationship. Why isn't this on the side emphasizing interpersonal relationships since it is human to human?

The most primordial relationship we know of is that between humans and God. That is why honoring parents is a commandment on the Human-God side of the tablets. Parents are partners with God in creating a child. And parents are supposed to mirror the way God is with us: loving us through our struggles and imperfections and guiding us to become all that we can be. God doesn't expect us to give back - only to appreciate all that we've been given and to pay it forward, just like a healthy parent to a child. In fact, our ability to perceive, feel and express gratitude begins with the quality of our early relationships. If we were given unconditional love and acceptance growing up, it is easier to feel appreciation for and connection with people and with God. If love was withheld or conditional, it actually makes it harder for us as adults to both accept help and express appreciation when help is offered because that's a vulnerable place for us.

The psychological foundation of this idea is called "attachment theory." John Bowlby, the first attachment theorist, describes attachment as a "lasting psychological connectedness between human beings." The central theme of attachment theory is that primary caregivers who are available and responsive to an infant's needs allow the child to develop a sense of security. The infant learns that the caregiver is dependable, which creates a secure base for the child to then go out and explore the world.

Because parents are our initial authority figures, the nature of our relationship with them can extend to all authority figures. That is one reason why children who lack proper attachment due to abuse, neglect or trauma will frequently display disorders such as oppositional defiant disorder (ODD), conduct disorder (CD), or post-traumatic stress disorder (PTSD). That lack of respect for and ability or desire to connect to authority figures can extend to our view of and connection to God.

Justice and Lambert (1986) compared the words adults used to describe their childhood recollections of their parents with their current perceptions of God. Those with the most negative image of their parents had the most negative image of God. Birky and Ball (1987) found that 18- to 21-year-olds' concepts of God were influenced by images of both mother and father, but the image of their idealized parent was closer to their God-image than that of the non idealized parent. These findings indicate that both positive and negative conceptions of parents influence children's concepts of God.[29]

Regardless of your emotional point, there is always room for growth! Shlomo Ibn Aderet, a 13th century Biblical and Talmudic scholar known as the Rashba, explains that the words "Blessed art thou our Lord" which introduce traditional blessings mean: "You, Lord, are the source of all blessings."[30] Every skill, talent, ability, that we have comes from the Infinite. The Talmud, recognizing how easy it is for us to forget or ignore this reality, teaches that one should try to recite these words 100 times a day to remind ourselves and to feel constant appreciation for the Divine gifts that have been bestowed upon us.

Acknowledging and expressing appreciation to the Divine source for your unique gifts is a powerful step towards the healthy egotism necessary to live life with presence. What solidifies this awareness into a well-formed habit of gratitude is repeated externalization of those thoughts. That is one of the true purposes of prayer; to give us a daily structure to express gratitude, appreciation, and awareness, remind us of our presence, and connect us to the Infinite.

Healthy egotism says "I am important and you are important". Unhealthy egotism says "I have to be important. Make me feel important." When you live from a soul perspective, you honor others as you honor yourself because you recognize that everyone has a piece of the Divine within them. In the spiritual world, there are no stratifications and no objective heights to reach. There is only each person from their own starting place with their own tools and resources, striving to be the highest version of themselves. There is no "more important" in soul terms. There is only human to human; Divine to Divine, soul to soul.

Recognizing the inherent importance in each of us is healthy egotism.

[Atara] *When I owned my own wellness business, I used to get calls (I still do!) from women interested in doing similar work to what I was doing. I never hesitated to share my knowledge and experience and do whatever I could to help them get started in their businesses. I had a number of people say to me over the years, "aren't you afraid of creating competition?" My answer was always the same. In human terms, we see resources as finite. The more you have, the less there is for me. In God's world, the pie is infinite. There is more than enough to go around. More than that, I believe with a full heart that I have exactly what I am supposed to have to fulfill my purpose and you have exactly what you are supposed to have to fulfill yours. I do not believe that I or anyone else will ever suffer for helping another person succeed. And I don't believe I ever did!*

Ethics of our Fathers teaches: "If I am not for myself then who will be for me? And if I am only for myself then what am I?" (1:14)

You have the power to find that perfect balance. And the key to doing so is presence and self-awareness.

It's time to step into YOUR own greatness.

HOW TO SOUL

CHAPTER FIVE

HOW WE MAKE DECISIONS

Hall of Fame baseball player Cal Ripken Jr. was named best shortstop of the 20th century, earning all star status in 19 out of his 21 seasons. Cal epitomized consistency, playing in a record 2,632 consecutive baseball games. That's over 16 seasons without missing a game.

But Ripken had a serious challenge. Shortstops are responsible for balls hit in a very wide space on the infield - one that runs between second and third base - a larger section of field than for any other position.. As a result, the shortstop is usually a shorter player who can move and react very quickly to field the ball. Due to his 6 ft 4 in (1.93 m), 225 lb (102 kg) body, Cal had to figure out how to overcome this height disadvantage. His thoughtful approach was part and parcel of how he became the greatest shortstop of the 20th century. What was that approach?

Cal answers: "I like to learn their hitters and our pitchers…I'm not blessed with the kind of range a lot of shortstops have. The way I have success is, I guess, by thinking."[31] Author George Will calls it "using his head" to make up for his physical limitations.

Before every game, Ripken would analyze the specific dynamics of each player in order to better anticipate where the ball would be likely to be hit for any given play. Then before each pitch he would ask himself questions like, what pitch is his pitcher throwing? How does that specific batter hit that pitch in that situation? If there are runners on base, where might that batter be trying to hit the ball? What is the texture of the grass and how will that impact the ball's movement? All this helped Cal anticipate the outcome of every pitch - if the ball is likely to go to his left, to his right, behind where he is playing, or in front of him. And he would move in that direction before the batter even hits the ball.

In Will's words, "assuming an average of 130 pitches per game over a 162-game season, Ripken tenses, rocks forward on the balls of his feet and begins to lean or move toward the infield grass, or to one side or the other, 21,000 times each season ."

What made Cal the greatest ever was not only his attention to detail. It was knowing himself. Cal wanted to play shortstop. He also knew he was at a disadvantage because of his height. If you were in Cal's place, what would you have done? Would you have given up on your dream of playing shortstop? Would you have just plowed forward and hoped for the best? Would you have gotten down on yourself or frustrated by things you can't control, like your size? Or would you have done what Cal did and made a conscious decision to figure out another way to be the best?

We make hundreds of decisions each day from significant to small. And yet how often do we look at how we make decisions? Cal took a more intellectual approach to decision-making to build his success. Others may take a more intuitive or experiential approach. What is critical is understanding success in life is much more likely when we make decisions consciously and mindfully. Making decisions on autopilot can lead to suboptimal results and sets us up for making decisions based on outside influences rather than from our own values, beliefs, and resources.

THE POWER TO CHOOSE

God created Man, the fusion of a soul and a body, "in His image" (Genesis 1:27). While the soul on its own is divine in nature, how is the physical, finite human being, bound by space and time, created in the "image" of the Creator? Numerous biblical commentaries explain that there is one, primary way in which the human experience embodies the divine: the power of choice.

CHAPTER FIVE: HOW WE MAKE DECISIONS

The essence of God is His ability to create and give through the power of decision making. It is that aspect of the Infinite that is the essence of the soul.

It is your ability to choose, to act beyond instinct, beyond habit, that represents your Godliness and is your defining trait as a human being.

Humans are the most complex beings in creation - intellectual, emotional, physical and spiritual. That means that how we make decisions can be complicated. Every decision is impacted by what we feel, what we have learned and experienced, and what we believe about ourselves and the world around us. To help us navigate the myriad of daily choices, most of us have some kind of compass that informs our decisions. Sometimes that compass is subconscious such as when we lack self-awareness or operate by habit. Sometimes the compass is external, such as pleasing others or acting out. Others may choose a core value as their compass such as family or religion or career. What if your soul is your compass? What does that look like? How do you access it when faced with a decision?

"It is impossible for us to imagine a human being whose soul is not torn. Only an inanimate object is whole. A human being is full of opposing desires, an inner war that rages inside constantly. A person's entire struggle is to unify the torn parts of his or her soul through a greater vision that includes everything. Only then will one move toward harmony." - Abraham Isaac Kook[32]

This challenge applies to all aspects of life and decision making.

You want to lose weight, but you love to eat. You want to express yourself, but you are afraid of being judged. You want to be healthier but you don't like exercise. You have bills you can't pay but you want that new phone. You want to take care of yourself, but you are accustomed to taking care of others. You want to love yourself, but don't know if you deserve it.

We've all experienced wanting more than one thing at the same time. Ambivalence is part of the human condition. But how do we resolve that ambivalence? Understanding and accounting for how we make decisions has everything to do with the quality and outcome of our lives. Yet most of us travel through our days unaware of our own decision-making processes, why and how we choose what we do, and how we can make better choices for ourselves.

King Solomon refers to this as walking "in pitch darkness, they do not know upon what they stumble." (Proverbs 14:16) 18th century mystic and philosopher Moses Haim Luzatto explains this to mean that human beings hurt themselves by going through life without being aware of the decisions that they are making. They are like a person walking along a highway blindfolded or along a ditch-lined path at night. A simple decision to turn to the right or to the left can have significant consequences. So it is with decisions we make on a regular basis.

We make hundreds, if not thousands, of decisions a day. Some of those decisions are small with negligible consequences, like having coffee or tea or wearing your red shoes or your black boots. Others are more significant, relating to work, relationships, and setting priorities. Like the strokes of a clay sculptor, every decision we make shapes us in some small way. Luzatto posits that "every act that we do" can bring us closer to who we are supposed to be or distance us from it. Yes, even ordering food and choosing what to wear can be a pause for thought to analyze if any damaging or negative motives are involved or to notice something positive about our thought process for these mundane choices. Luzatto says that we should "run like fire" from that which distances us from the ultimate goal and to "chase after and grab" anything which brings us closer to the goal "like metal to a magnet."[33]

YOUR SOUL'S MISSION

Making better decisions for yourself involves listening to the voice of your soul as we explained above. But it all requires an understanding of what is driving your decisions - which priorities and values you want to honor, which behavioral "muscles" you want to strengthen, how much risk you are willing to take. Understanding your 'why' is also important.

As we go through life, our goals and priorities may change. The choices, behaviors or thought patterns that protected us, defined us, satisfied us in the past, may no longer serve us in the present.

For example, many of us developed coping skills that were necessary for 'survival' in our younger years - skills that were adaptive at the time of development. Maybe you learned that being quiet and out of site protected you at an earlier time. Or maybe you turned to food or substances to numb emotional pain. But as you get older, you realize that what once protected you has become maladaptive - it is creating stress in your life and is negatively impacting your decisions. The first step to change is an awareness of what you want change to look like. Once you have an image of where you want to go, you can begin to train yourself through small decisions at first.

Luzatto reminds us that a person "must determine what he is aiming for and how to achieve this - in all his labors throughout his lifetime."[34]

Organizations have mission statements to focus and guide their decision-making. Without having a clear statement of value and purpose, companies cannot succeed in a competitive world. As human beings we are not so different. Without a clear sense of what a whole life looks and feels like for each of us, we make decisions based on fleeting and changeable factors such as mood, emotional state, or peer pressure or simply fall back into the rut of habit, without even making actual decisions. In that scenario, forward motion is random and sporadic rather than steady and intentional.

The Talmud teaches that we have no control over a number of factors that have significant influence on our lives including who our parents are, the families and environment we are born into, and our natural talents and skills. The one thing we do have control over is the decisions that we make with the lot that we are handed.[35]

To assist us in this process, we can create and rely on a personal mission statement, a whole life vision, to guide us. It is not about creating the perfect life, if that were to even exist. It's about creating a life of consciousness and intention. A life of eyes open and heart open, creating and embracing possibility.

EXERCISE #4
YOUR SOUL'S MISSION STATEMENT

There is no greater joy than knowing and fulfilling your soul purpose in life. This exercise is designed to help you discover your unique spiritual mission. Combine your answers to the following prompts with the answers from the Seven Days of Soul [Exercise #2, chapter 3] to create your soul mission statement.

Write in the first person and make statements about the future you hope to achieve. Write the statements as if you are already making them happen in your life. Some experts recommend keeping your vision statements 50 words or less, but it is more useful to fully articulate the vision you want for your life and your future, rather than limiting yourself by the word count.

List five or six of your most important values:

Examples: Accomplishment, Accountability, Accuracy, Ambition, Challenge, Collaboration, Competency, Courage, Credibility, Dedication, Dependability, Dignity, Diversity, Efficiency, Empathy, Empowerment, Enjoyment/Fun, Equality, Excellence, Flexibility, Honesty, Improvement, Independence, Individuality, Innovativeness, Integrity, Loyalty, Optimism, Persistency, Quality, Respect, Responsibility, Security, Service, Stewardship, Teamwork, Wisdom.

If an alien was to watch your life from above, what would it think your values are based on your actions? What do you need to work on to begin to live more into your values?

What triggers feelings of fear/constriction for you? What gives you a feeling of love/expansion?

What are the five things you most enjoy doing? Be honest. These are five things without which your weeks, months, and years would feel incomplete.

1.

2.

3.

4.

5.

What three things must you do every single day to feel fulfilled?

1.

2.

3.

If you never had to work another day in your life, how would you spend your time?

When your life is ending, what will you regret not doing, seeing, or achieving?

Sample soul mission statements:

To use my gifts of intelligence, charisma and serial optimism to cultivate an atmosphere of abundance in my home and my classroom.

My mission in life is not merely to survive, but to thrive; and to do so with some passion, some compassion, some humor, and some style (Maya Angelou)

To have fun in my journey through life and to learn from my mistakes. (Richard Branson)

To live life with integrity and empathy, and be a positive force in the lives of others. (Amy Ziari)

Improve lives. The concept of improving lives runs through the center of everything I do. (Will Smith)

I shall not fear anyone on Earth. I shall fear only God. I shall not bear ill will toward anyone. I shall not submit to injustice from anyone. I shall conquer untruth by truth. And in resisting untruth, I shall put up with all suffering. (Gandhi)

Write your soul mission statement here:

YOUR BUILT-IN MOBILEYE

Your soul's mission statement is like the lane you are driving in on the highway of life. The lane markers establish the pathway that you have chosen. When you veer from your lane, the Mobileye system sets off an alarm to make sure you remain in your lane. That beeping noise doesn't stop your car from leaving the lane. It just alerts you that you are going off course. You can choose to heed the warning and adjust your steering to stay in your lane or you can allow your car to slide into the next lane or straddle between the two lanes. It's your choice to make.

All of us are wired with our own personal, internal Mobileye system. Deep inside we know when we are veering away from our mission. If you are in touch with yourself, sensors are going off in a variety of formats - emotional, psychological, and spiritual - urging you to get back on course. You can choose to ignore those signs and allow yourself to drift into a different lane. But even if you choose that approach, at least you are aware and can turn the steering wheel to bring yourself back into your path.

There are some people who get annoyed by the beeping sound of the Mobileye system. So, they choose the option of turning it off. This puts them at great risk since there are times when lack of attention can lead a car out of its lane and into devastating consequences. Far too many people choose to turn off their natural Mobileye. They don't want to be bothered with the uncomfortable feeling that comes with self-reflection and the nagging inner-voice telling them to stay on course. Or they have learned not to trust the warning system. They turn off the sensors and don't allow for any internal messaging telling them that they should get back on course or at least be aware that they are veering off course. The tragic result is living a life without the peace and inner calm that accompanies living with focus and meaning.

Let's go back to our caretaker scenario.

What does the caretaker have to be aware of to start focusing on her own well being? What might need to shift? Her inner dialogue? Her self-definition? What about her values and priorities? Is she looking for wholesale change or just modification? What is driving her desire for change now? What does success look like? What is the end game? These self-reflections are the foundation for change because they anchor your desires in meaningful outcomes. In other words, the vision of a better future becomes the energy source required to choose a new option in the face of old habits.

DECISION POINT

In the world of personal development individual change can revolve around one moment in space and time that gets repeated over and over - the point of decision or the point of action.

[**Atara**] *I have a coaching client, Sarah, who wants to change her pattern of emotional eating. Every time Sarah feels a strong and uncomfortable emotion, she turns to comfort foods to soothe the pain. But her weight is creeping up, her energy level is dropping, and she is worried about her long term physical health. She wants to change her eating habits and to find alternatives to dealing with strong emotions* *that don't undermine her wellbeing in the broader sense Through our coaching sessions, Sarah states a goal for herself that in moments of strong emotion, instead of turning to the kitchen, she will sit down, take four deep breaths and name the emotion. Once she names the emotion, she will spend 10 minutes journaling about what triggered that emotional reaction.*

Every time Sarah has an emotional reaction, she has the opportunity to choose the new behavior or slide effortlessly into the old behavior. To choose the new behavior and begin to build the new habit, she will need to catch herself being triggered. She will then have to pause and engage her conscious mind and make a choice. It is in that brief moment - between trigger and reaction - where Sarah can decide to do what she's always done or choose something different.

Choosing something different requires energy and awareness. By contrast, operating by habit is effortless, even comforting. The source of the energy to make a different choice is to deeply connect to the why of a new behavior. In this case, Sarah needs to be crystal clear how making the choice to breathe and journal instead of eating her feelings will give her more of what she really wants now and in the future.

[Atara] *I know that if I react in the moment of a strong emotion, I am going to say things too strongly, too direct, and sometimes harsh. It may be honest and feel good to get off my chest, but it can be unproductive. I often find myself wishing that I had taken a beat, stopped to breathe and center myself, and respond from a calmer and clearer place. At many points in my life, reacting strongly and directly protected me and created a kind of armor for myself. But I understand now that it's not a way of reacting that serves me best in the long run. I want to feel good about how I respond and in a way that I admire in others when I see it - with dignity and respect for myself and the person with whom I am speaking. I want to become proficient at communicating my feelings and needs clearly while honoring the other person's experience and humanity. Life gives me ample opportunity to practice these skills. Yet, every time I hit that crossroads, I have to consciously choose again. I have to tap into the image of who I want to be and what that version of myself means to me to make a better choice than I would have in the past. When it comes to making decisions that differ from habitual responses, you have to tap into self-awareness and recommit to your higher values each time.*

In the words of Dr. Stephen Covey, author of the landmark book *7 Habits of Highly Effective People*,[36] all things are created twice. The first creation is in your mind - the mental image of what you want. The second creation is the physical expression of that mental image or vision. Covey calls this second of seven habits, "begin with the end in mind" and is the foundation of the concept of goal setting. Without having a clear vision of where you want to go, you will end up wherever the wind takes you, as opposed to a location of your desire and choosing.

At the heart of this decision making process is awareness and courage. We have to be willing to look at how we've been living and decide if we want to continue down the path or turn off onto a new road. If we choose the former, it is with awareness that we are doing so. If we choose the latter, it is with hope and faith and a desire for something other than what we have or what we think we must accept.

Kalonymus Kalman Shapira, a 20th-century Hasidic master who was murdered in the Holocaust, taught that true awareness is not limited to the external world but must also be applied inwardly. He emphasized that people often filter out or lose trust in their inner perceptions, making self-discovery a gradual process that requires patience and reflection. According to his teachings, developing a deeper connection to one's inner world involves noting personal insights as they arise and allowing them to shape a renewed sense of self. Through this process, one can begin to open the door to a richer, more expansive inner experience. [37]

EVEN WITH THE BEST INTENTIONS...
WHAT GETS IN OUR WAY

Creating a vision is a statement of hope and potential: we want more for ourselves, our lives. It is a statement that we are willing to dream, to reach, to consider new possibilities. It also means that to actualize that vision, we have to make the effort to bring the changes about. It is in this space that we start to feel the tug of resistance. What are the obstacles we face when we set out - with the best of intentions - to do better, to be better. What gets in our way? And how can we navigate those challenges in a productive and positive way?

A significant factor in how we make decisions revolves around our inner dialogue. We all have a constant stream of thoughts running through our minds like a ticker tape in Times Square. The thoughts are so constant and so familiar that we often aren't even conscious of them. In happier, calmer moments the inner dialogue can be a curious observer. But often, especially when important decisions need to be made or our mood is low, the inner voice is the skeptical naysayer, fear monger or disempowering critic. We all have moments of self-doubt and insecurity, but when the critical voice keeps us from growing, keeps us small and stuck and fearful and doubting, it's time to take a look at how that voice is serving our lives.

The voice of the inner critic can take a number of forms. It may sound like "I can't do this" or "I'm not good enough" or "I'll never change" or "I should be less selfish." Or it may sow seeds of fear like "don't trust anyone (most of all yourself)" or "don't let up if you want to succeed." The inner critic may demand perfection (impossible), convince you that worrying is productive and that anxiety and guilt have value. It may make the case that denying your needs and emotions will make them go away, or that once you get all your ducks in a row, your life will be happy and fulfilling. In short, the inner critic uses shame, blame, judgment and fear to weigh you down and prevent you from soaring.

Medieval rabbinic authority Jacob ben Asher, known as "the Tur," writes about an inner "voice" that encourages inertia and weighs us down.[38] The voice posits, playing off Newton's First Law of Motion, that an object at rest should remain at rest and looks for ways to undermine our determination to take action in the moment.

We all have this voice. Having it is not the problem. Mistaking that voice for our true selves and making decisions based on our inner critic is where we run into trouble. Thoughts are not facts.

Because development of our thinking patterns is generally subconscious, negative thought patterns become habitual, to the extent that we can no longer distinguish them from our true selves. These limiting beliefs preclude our ability to fully experience, appreciate and enjoy the gift of life and to be as successful as we can be. They are the voices in our head that make us question ourselves - our worth, intentions, abilities and goodness - and narrow our field of vision to focus on all our (real or perceived) failabilities.

If we are trying to connect with our soul, we need to take a step back when we hear the riffing of negative inner chatter. The voice of the soul reflects its very nature: unbounded, striving, expansive, full of possibility. The voice of the inner critic is punitive, shaming, and limiting. By definition then, these two inner influences are mutually exclusive. So if you're listening to the inner critic, in effect you are obstructing the voice of the soul.

THE VIRTUE OF VIGILANCE

So how can we create space between our inner critic and our truest selves? How can we amplify the voice of our essence, the part of our inner world that knows and believes in our potential and our greatness? Luzatto calls this "the virtue of vigilance," using awareness to resist operating by rote and habit. When we run on automatic pilot, it can render us captive to our inner critic, thereby depriving ourselves of all the positive and authentic good available to us in life.

Luzatto teaches that the mechanism for this awareness is to set aside time for daily self reflection. *"I see a need for a person to carefully examine his ways and to weigh them daily in the manner of the great merchants who constantly evaluate all of their business dealings so that they do not miscalculate (and lose money.) He should set aside definite times and hours for this weighing so that it is not a fortuitous matter, but one which is conducted with the greatest regularity; for it yields rich returns."* Luzatto suggests that this daily reflection should include an assessment of the path which we want to follow, since this can also be modified as we experience the trials and tribulations of our life journey. Through daily reflection about our life's mission alongside a daily review of that day's challenges and decisions, *"he will come to consider whether or not his deeds travel along this path."*

Practicing this "virtue of vigilance" is the first line of defense against the inner critic. It puts the self-saboteur into perspective as it appears against a much larger background of meaning and purpose. In this light, the inner critic can be seen for what it is, a small part of you with a big voice.

This act of mindfulness also illuminates another antidote to the inner critic: self-compassion and empathy.

SELF COMPASSION AND EMPATHY

Self-compassion is the choice to be gentle and forgiving to yourself in moments of struggle and vulnerability instead of shaming, guilting, and criticizing yourself. According to Kristen Neff, associate professor in the University of Texas at Austin's department of educational psychology, self-compassion has three elements: self-kindness, a sense of common humanity, and mindfulness. Self-kindness reminds us to put the hammer away and stop beating ourselves as an attempt at 'punishment' or motivation. It allows us to be human and builds resilience by giving us permission to make mistakes and learn from them as part of the human experience and growth process. It's adjusting our perspective to seeing mistakes as learning opportunities rather than failures. By contrast, self-criticism breaks us down and lowers our bandwidth to cope with challenges effectively.[39]

Next time you are faced with a challenge or difficult decision, ask yourself, "What do I need to hear right now to express kindness to myself?" Alternatively, what would you say to someone you love if they were struggling with the same choice or situation?

A sense of common humanity means internalizing that every human being struggles - no one gets out of this life unscathed. When we face difficult decisions with the knowledge that we all have strengths and weaknesses, that we all face challenges, it creates space for self-compassion. It is at these crossroads where we can build our self-confidence by honoring our inner world and coming out stronger on the other side.

Mindfulness is tapping into our souls, understanding our true selves, and keeping our dreams and goals top of mind when making decisions. The voice of the soul and the voice of the inner critic are mutually exclusive. The voice of the soul is never critical and judgmental. So if you're listening to the inner critic, you are obstructing the voice of the soul.

The next time you have a decision to make, whether it's what to wear or which job offer to accept, observe your inner dialogue. Don't judge what you hear. Just listen. What are the words of your inner critic? What is the tone? Does it sound like the voice of someone else you know? What are the underlying messages? Are they fear, survival, control, anger, passivity, incompetence, self loathing?

It can be helpful to personify your inner critic. How does it look in your mind's eye? Is it a person? A thing? An amorphous blob? A talking head? A creature? A sound? Giving your inner critic an identity can help you see it as the 'other' that it is; as a part of your thought process but not a reflection of your essence or your true potential. And it's a part you can change through self-compassion and mindfulness.

As you begin observing your inner critic, notice how it plays into your decision-making. How much weight do you give your inner critic in your daily choices? How does it impact your ability to move forward? Journaling your observations can be a powerful tool to increase awareness of your inner dialogue and its impact on your quality of life.

MEDITATION #3
MAKING DECISIONS

1. Call to mind an issue that you have to make a decision about that has some import in your life.
2. Choose a comfortable place to sit - a location which inherently brings you some level of calm. If you don't have one, you may need to try a few places and see how they feel.
3. Select a song to listen to that relaxes you and gives you a sense of peace.. It can be any type of music. You can play it for a few minutes or as many times as you need to feel relaxed.
4. Once the music has relaxed you, spend 2-3 minutes taking deep breaths. Focus on fully inhaling and exhaling. You can do this with the music on or off.

5. Think about the decision that you have to make. Tune out all outside noise and gently focus your inner eye on your core self. Ask your inner self what it wants to do. Let it talk to you. Hear what it's telling you.

Write down what your inner knowing tells so you can have it to reflect on when you are distracted by noise inside or outside of yourself.

A WORD ABOUT HABITS

"Bad habits start off like a spider web and end up being like the ropes of a wagon." (Talmud Bavli, Tractate Sukkah 52a)

The Talmud is teaching that habits start small, almost unnoticeable, but when they aren't addressed properly they grow to become dominating forces in our lives.

What makes habits so powerful? Because they are automatic. Habits require little to no thought or planning. They don't require willpower. They are built into your schedule and built into your life. In short, habits are behaviors that have morphed into who you are. They are part and parcel of your lifestyle.

The automaticity of habits can work for you or against you, depending on what you are trying to accomplish. On the positive side, if self-care is a habit and not just a set of behaviors - like eating healthfully, sleeping eight hours a night, moving your body daily - you can operate on cruise control and still be taking care of yourself. On the flip side, if you are trying to make healthier choices, you may run up against old habits and patterns that get in the way. Since habit trumps willpower, how can you make progress in the long run? There is a way to hack the system! It isn't a shortcut or a quick fix. But it does take advantage of current habits to build new, more healthful habits. And it's called stacking.

Here is how stacking health behaviors works. Let's assume that you want to jump start a morning exercise routine. Let's also assume that you are in the habit of making your lunch for work the night before. Since you are already in the groove of preparing for the next day, when you make lunch, you decide to lay out your exercise clothes for the morning. You are stacking a new behavior on top of a habit. With time and repetition, the two actions become one 'bedtime routine.'

Let's pick another example. You would like to learn to meditate. But you just can't get yourself to sit down and be still for even a few minutes. Too much to do. Too much in your head. Too buzzy. As soon as your alarm goes off, bleary-eyed and barely able to see in front of you, you manage to find the kitchen. Your autopilot also manages to find the coffee and the pourover cup. Soon your daily brew is in your hand.

If you were to stack the new desired behavior on top of this well-worn coffee habit, it might look like using the four minutes while your coffee is brewing to meditate. Your coffee is your reward for practicing (and stacking) the new behavior of meditation.

The key to successful long term change is to recognize that the goal is to create new habits, not just new behaviors. Behaviors outside of the context of the rest of your life just sit on the surface of daily living and often rely on chance, willpower or perfect circumstances to make them happen. Habit is effortless.

The difference between a behavior and a habit? Repetition.

It can take several months for a new behavior to become a habit (that '21 days to a new habit' rumor isn't supported by research). It doesn't have to be repeated daily but it should be repeated as often as you would like it to show up as a habit. Want to work out three times a week? Which current habit can you stack the new behavior on top of that you do at least three times a week? Start with five minutes of exercise if need be, three times a week. The purpose is to train the behavior, not the exact details. Your goal is to create a habit!

There is one more technique when it comes to stacking and building new habits: combining something pleasurable with a less-pleasurable new behavior. Trying to get better at food prep for the week but don't like cleaning and chopping all those vegetables? Listen to a podcast, TED talk or music, or talk on the phone with a friend or family member while you are food prepping. Don't like exercise but love socializing? How can you set up your exercise to combine the two?

Be very wary of the word 'should' in this process. "Should" means the change is driven by an external expectation rather than an internal driver. That makes change far less compelling when we come up against resistance.

We also have to be real - very real - about how important support, self-awareness and self compassion are in the change process. It's also important to know that setbacks are not simply to be accepted but to be expected.

Please see APPENDIX A on page 159 for additional guidance regarding finding the courage to make significant decisions.

EXERCISE #5
CHANGING BEHAVIORS

1. Make a list of 3 or 4 behaviors that you would like to change
2. Rate those behaviors on a scale of 1-10 in terms of how excited you would be to successfully make changes in that area of your life with 1 being not at all excited and 10 being very excited.
3. Now rate those same behaviors on a scale of 1-10 based on which would have the most significant positive impact on your life if you successfully make changes in that area.
4. Based on your ratings, select the behavior or habit which receives the highest collective number.
5. Choose a specific time of day when you would like to work on that behavior, ideally during a time that you are likely to have the greatest success. For example, if you are trying to be a more positive thinker, you may want to select a time of day when you have the most energy rather than when you are exhausted, to work on the new behavior.
6. What other habit or productive behavior do you engage in at that time of day that you can stack with the new behavior?
7. Outline the specific action or behavior you want to work on. Get granular about this: What will you do? Where will you do it? How long will you do it for? What day/s of the week? Between what hours?

8. Consider what you need to set yourself up for success. Do you need any specific resources? Do you need to share your plan with anyone in your life whom it may impact?
9. Create accountability for yourself. You can log your successes in your journal or on a calendar. You can also recruit a friend who can help hold you accountable. Every time you practice the new behavior at the time you planned, record it as a success. Once you reach your behavior goal, reward yourself in some way.
10. If you miss a practice session, reflect on what got in the way and determine how you will address that obstacle the next time you face it.

Your body and soul were placed into circumstances and environments in this world that were out of your control.

But life choices are yours to make.

HOW TO SOUL

INTRODUCTION

TO CHAPTERS 6-9

The soul is our eternal and essential self. But the soul in this world lives in a body. What is the relationship between the two? How are we to relate to our physical selves? Where do our mind and emotions fit in the picture? Are we supposed to be ascetics and live a life of material denial to achieve our true potential? Is happiness dependent only on the degree to which we care for our souls?

In *Ethics of our Fathers*,[40] a 2,000 year old compilation of ethical teachings, we learn that without physical sustenance, we cannot properly focus on spiritual growth, and that if there is only physical sustenance and no spiritual growth, we cannot thrive. Fast forward to 1943 to the development of Maslow's hierarchy of need by U.S. psychologist Abraham Maslow. Maslow posits that people have five sets of needs, which come in a particular order. As each level of needs is satisfied, the desire to fulfill the next set kicks in. At the bottom of Maslow's pyramid are the most primary needs of safety and survival, including food, water, warmth, rest, and shelter. By extension, we can call that physical wellbeing. Once these basic physical needs are met, we can move up the hierarchy to focus on psychological needs, followed by self-fulfillment needs including self-actualization and achieving one's full potential. In Maslow's thinking then, physical wellbeing is a prerequisite for spiritual actualization.

Maimonides, a 12th century scholar and philosopher, addresses the relationship between our psychological and emotional states and our spiritual health. He writes that the highest level of spiritual connection in biblical times was prophecy which required that the prophet be in a positive mental state to receive God's direct communications. Maimonides says that prophecy "could not rest upon a person when he is sad or languid, but only when he is happy."[41] Happiness is fed by an eye for the good and a sense of gratitude both of which generate feelings of spiritual connectedness. In Chinese philosophy, these are Yang emotions and represent expansiveness, lightness, creativity and warmth.

While authentic happiness is a catalyst for spiritual connection, it is also possible to feel the tug of the soul when we are in deep pain or when we feel desperate and out of control. Thus the origin of the expression, "there are no atheists in a foxhole" and the "let go and let God" motto of 12 step recovery programs. When we feel helpless or impotent to change a painful situation, engaging with God and our soul gives us hope, hope that we can be pulled from the abyss in time to make new choices for ourselves, to grow, to be better, to seek more goodness. In fact, our most painful life challenges could be could be given to us by God expressly for this purpose - to nudge (or sometimes push) us to becoming more spiritually connected beings.

We all go in and out of positive and negative emotions at varying degrees. And while an acute challenge can wake us up spiritually, long term negative emotional states can have a deleterious effect on our spiritual growth and connection. Anger, fear, hopelessness, sadness, and depression create spiritual drag and can be difficult to uproot without a concerted effort to do so. In Chinese philosophy, these are yin emotions and represent darkness, contraction, passivity and absorption.

So what does this say about caring for our physical and emotional selves in the context of our souls? The body is the vehicle by which the soul expresses itself in this world, the world of "*asiya*" meaning "doing" in Hebrew. Just as a car without wheels can't get down the road no matter how fast the engine, so too our soul expression is hampered by illness or disease of any kind - physical or mental. When we feel physically well, when our mind and mood are in a positive state, we have the bandwidth and capacity to focus on the spiritual work that we want to do. When we are ill or stressed or drained physically or mentally, it is very challenging to prioritize our spiritual wellbeing.

Observant Jews say a prayer called *Asher Yatzar* ("He Who created") every time they use the bathroom, thanking God for creating human physiology with profound wisdom. Every part of our bodies - those that we are conscious of and those that we are not - must work well and together for us to be able to function optimally in the world. That balance is more delicate than we think. The prayer states that if any small part of ourselves is blocked, ruptured, or not functioning properly, "it would be impossible to survive and to stand before You for even one moment."

These words, recited many times a day, remind us of the continuous miracle of life and the incredible blessing we receive when we live free of pain and discomfort. That freedom creates space for us to seek higher ground - to reach in and up towards our spiritual potential.

[Atara] *In my work with cancer patients, when they are in the depths of treatment and side effects, a successful day may be when they have the energy to talk or walk to a different room in the house. Those are significant accomplishments. Once they are on the road to recovery, when their bodies are stronger again, it is then that they can begin to emotionally and spiritually process and reflect on what they want to learn from or become as a result of the cancer experience.*

With this background, we turn to four pathways - nature, music, movement, and food. Each one of these has the capacity to play a significant role in building and supporting our bodies, our minds, and our emotions, thereby enabling and empowering us to lead more soulful lives.

HOW TO SOUL

CHAPTER SIX

NATURE AND SOUL

Daniel Elice was a typical uninspired young professional searching for his purpose in life, caught up in the rat race of earning a living. A trip to Colorado changed his life.

"While on a hike in the Rocky Mountains, the group took a break at the top. I walked to a quiet spot and gazed across at the beautiful landscape. I felt relaxed, happy and content. Nothing else in the world mattered at that moment. The trip was over in the blink of an eye, and I was quickly back to the grind - working, and working more hours than before. At the same time, I was craving the feelings I experienced on the peak of the mountain. I was craving that state of contentment. I was craving the sense of purpose and sense of ownership of my own life. I was craving that freedom. And I was craving that connection with God that I recently experienced. Although back to work, I was still on a Colorado Denver high and the inspiration from the trip returned with me. I began to read two books on discovering one's unique purpose as well as finding inner peace in life…The Colorado trip reminded me that there is bigger purpose in one's life than what we experience physically in our day-to-day lives."

Daniel was struggling with a number of difficult emotions that many of us can relate to:

fatigue, stress, burnout, disconnection from himself, work-life imbalance, lack of spiritual inspiration, purpose and meaning.

Experiencing the beauty and vastness of nature allowed him to shed the negative emotions and tap into entirely different parts of himself. He felt relaxed, happy, content, connected, and peaceful. Tapping into his memory of his time in the mountains also inspired his spiritual journey as he sought to create more meaning and discover his unique purpose.

[Dov] *I can very much relate to Daniel's epiphany in the Rockies. I grew up praying three times as a day as has been practiced for thousands of years in traditional Judaism. I don't think I ever felt a connection to God while doing so throughout my childhood. And, then, my family drove across the United States during the summer between 10th and 11th grade. When we woke up early to pray at sunrise while visiting the Grand Canyon, I suddenly felt God. I will never forget the moment. The beauty of the sun's rays beaming down on the vastness of the canyon led to an overwhelming feeling of spirituality and the Divine. For the first time in my life, at 16-years-old, I felt a connection to my Creator.*

Four-time NBA champion Klay Thompson of the Golden State Warriors regularly swims in the San Francisco Bay. At a press conference during the 2022 NBA Finals, a reporter asked him why he does this. Thompson explained:

"I just think the ocean has healing properties that a pool might not have, or a cool tub. Just to be immersed in nature like that, it really makes me happy. Your whole body feels so great when you get out of that cold water. Honestly, you just feel a little closer to God when you look up at the beautiful skies and you're just in the ocean...It really is my happy place."[42]

NATURE WALKS THE SOUL BACK HOME

Starting from Abraham who gazed up to the heavens and concluded that there must be a God,[43] to King David over 1,000 years later who sang, "The heavens declare the glory of God and the skies proclaim his handiwork" (Psalms 19:2), nature has long been a source of spiritual inspiration. Maimonides teaches that "When one reflects on God's wonderful creation and discerns and discovers the limitless wisdom contained therein, one is necessarily gripped by admiration and love for the Creator."[44] Maimonides's son, Rabbi Abraham, internalized his father's teachings, saying that "access to the enjoyment of the beauties of nature - meadows full of flowers, majestic mountains, flowing rivers" is "essential" for spiritual development.[45]

In the words of award-winning author Mary Davis, *"A walk in nature walks the soul back home."*[46]

What is it about nature that makes it such a game changer physically, emotionally and spiritually?

The vastness, beauty and diversity of nature inspires our most spiritual emotion: awe.

Awe is the feeling of great respect and wonder that is inspired by the sacred or sublime. The mental, spiritual and physical benefits of awe derive from a shift in five processes that benefit well-being—changes in neurophysiology, a diminished focus on the self, increased prosocial relationality, greater social integration, and a heightened sense of meaning.[47]

Nature is one of the most powerful and accessible sources of awe. Engaging with the natural world lightens our spirit, calms our nervous system, puts life in perspective, and fills us with a deep sense of pleasure when we witness such grandeur. It allows us to think more expansively and let go of things that pull us down. It opens the door to gratitude and to connecting to our souls.

Ralph Waldo Emerson summarizes awe and nature eloquently: *"In the woods, we return to reason and faith. There I feel that nothing can befall me in life—no disgrace, no calamity (leaving me my eyes), which nature cannot repair. Standing on the bare ground—my head bathed by the blithe air and uplifted into infinite space—all mean egotism vanishes. I become a transparent eyeball; I am nothing; I see all; the currents of the Universal Being circulate through me; I am part or parcel of God. The name of the nearest friend sounds then foreign and accidental; to be brothers, to be acquaintances, master or servant, is then a trifle and a disturbance. I am the lover of uncontained and immortal beauty".*[48]

10th century poet, Biblical scholar Abraham Ibn Ezra captured this beautifully in his poem entitled "God everywhere": *"Wherever I turn my eyes, around on Earth or to the heavens, I see you in the field of stars, I see You in the yield of the land, in every breath and sound, a blade of grass, a simple flower, an echo of Your holy Name."*[49]

[Atara] Spiritual but not religious. That is how I would describe myself from my earliest memories. I was a sensitive and soulful child without any real context for developing those sides of myself. But I naturally gravitated to nature for spiritual nourishment. I was fortunate to live in areas and be surrounded by people with a similar appreciation for the great outdoors. I grew up in Minnesota, went to college in the Green Mountains of western Massachusetts, went to graduate school near the Blue Ridge mountains of Kentucky, and wrote my graduate thesis at the East-West Center in Honolulu, HI. I was an avid hiker, camper, runner and general outdoorswoman. I ran outdoor leadership programs during summers and after graduating with a Master's in Public and Environmental Affairs, worked in the public housing neighborhoods of Washington DC and New York City as an urban greening specialist building flower and vegetable gardens with and for the residents. It was incredible to see the children's eyes alight when their vegetables appeared from seedlings almost overnight. The children were growing up in difficult circumstances, and working in the gardens was a healing outlet for them.

Nature for me is therapeutic, awe-inspiring and wholesome. But it is also my teacher. Nature is the great equalizer. It does not judge or discriminate. It welcomes everyone. The natural world also embodies presence. It isn't right or wrong. Nature just IS - exactly as it is created to be - exquisitely present in its beauty, diversity, power and symmetry. A witness to its own creation as well as to human history, it whispers the secrets of the universe. Even now as a religiously observant person, nature was and will always be for me my primary and most important connector to God and my soul.

Award winning author Dr. Ronald Bissell writes: "You will be taken on a solitary walk along a beach where you will experience the quiet observation of creatures and the rhythms of nature seen along the way. Through this walk you will find the unity found in all of creation. Like the sandpiper's dance with the waves, you will gently discover the essence of your soul in the beauty and harmony of spirit as it surrounds you. Through this quiet contemplation you will feel a sense of awe at the potential within each living creature - the potential to bring the experience of unity into the consciousness of the world."[50]

In the words of travel writer and poet Gretel Erlich, *"Everything in nature invites us constantly to be what we are."*

Nature's song

The inherent existence of spirituality in Creation is demonstrated further by an intriguing ancient work called "Perek Shira," Hebrew for "Chapter of Song." This text, at least 2,000 years old, contains Biblical verses of the "song lyrics" that are continuously "sung" by each aspect of the natural world. Commentaries explain that these songs impart spiritual lessons to us and serve as one of the channels of communication between God and humans as we try to navigate through life.

Chapter one contains the spiritual messages of the wilderness, the fields, and all bodies of water. For example, chapter one relates that the fields quote the verse "'God founded the land with wisdom" (Proverbs 3:19). This teaches that when we see a field it is an opportunity to reflect on the remarkable process involved with plowing, planting, and rainfall in order to produce crops - a process that demonstrates the Divine hand behind the fruits and vegetables that we eat. It also reminds us of the remarkable potential and capabilities that we have as human beings since God's "wisdom" created a world in which human beings partner with the Creator to further advance the world and the universe.

The second chapter teaches the spiritual lessons of the sun, moon, stars, clouds, lightning, rain, and dew. Chapter three reveals the spirituality that comes from trees, grass, vines, and crops that grow from the ground. Birds and fish share their spiritual angle in chapter four, chapters five and six teach the spiritual messages emanating from the rest of the animate world.

As an illustration, chapter five teaches that the elephant sings, "How great are Your deeds, God. Your thoughts are very deep." (Psalms 92:6) The "depth" the elephant sings about is the divine wisdom in its design. For example, given its size, it would be impossible for the elephant to hunt enough meat to sustain its massive body . Thus, it was created as herbivore who's food is plentiful and easy to find. Its trunk enables the elephant to reach the ground to eat in place of a long neck which would have made it vulnerable to predators. This, in turn, should remind us that we, too, have been given all the tools and skills we need to successfully achieve our unique purpose in the world.

Because each soul has a specific role to play in the world, God provides road maps for achieving that purpose. Perek Shira is one of those maps. It reminds us that we are part of a majestic tapestry known as "the universe" and that the design of nature holds secrets to our own potential. This expansive perspective can enable and empower us to connect to and activate the vast potential you possess. You are a soul and body with a unique role to play in the infinite beauty and grandeur of creation.

ASTRONAUTS AND THE BOOK OF JOB

The awe inspired by nature is perhaps most starkly experienced from outside of our terrestrial home. Numerous astronauts have spoken about the transformative experience they underwent in outer space. Apollo 14 astronaut Edgar Mitchell said, "Something happens to you out there. He describes an "interconnected euphoria" that comes from being in space and from seeing Earth from space. After his time in space, Mitchell founded Noetic Institute to research altered states of consciousness. Gene Cernan, who walked on the moon as part of the Apollo 17 mission, was inspired to feel that "There has to be somebody bigger than you, and bigger than me, and I mean this in a spiritual sense, not a religious sense." Apollo astronaut Russel Shcweikart's time in space led to his beginning transcendental meditation and to dedicating the rest of his life to volunteer work.[51]

The role that nature can play in changing the way we view life and ourselves brings to mind the words of Job, whose life story is recorded in the Book of Job. This man suffered immensely through his life: all of his children passed away, all his livestock died, he lost all his money, and his body was filled with painful sores. And despite it all, he maintained his faith that ultimately we are spiritual beings sent on a journey through this physical world. How did Job remain true to his spiritual self despite his terrible suffering?

One clue can be found in Chapter 12 where he reveals the clarity that he gleaned from nature:

"But ask now the animals, and they shall teach you; And the birds of the sky, and they shall tell you; Or speak to the Earth, and it shall teach you; And the fishes of the sea shall declare unto you; Who knows not among all these, That the hand of God has wrought this. In whose hand is the soul of every living thing, And the breath of all humanity. (12:7-10)

Aside from its ability to inspire spiritual recognition and growth, nature is also a path to healing, particularly healing a troubled mind. It can raise your spirits when you are down, help bring you calm when you are disturbed, and even help nurse you to physical health.

[Dov] *When things bother me, I know that being outside - especially in a beautiful place - will help me dig deep and connect to my deepest inner self. When I am really down or troubled and pained by life circumstances, I will often literally lie on the grass in my backyard late at night, when it's totally quiet, and just look at the sky. The stunning beauty and mystery of the sparkling stars hanging amidst the vastness of space, reminds me that there is so much that I don't understand and have to just accept. It also inspires me to reaffirm that there must be a Creator and that we are part of a broader plan which includes growth through pain and challenges. The feeling brings me so much comfort that I don't want it to end and have to force myself to go inside and leave that special place and moment. I do what I can to take that peace, calm, and clarity with me into my regular life schedule.*

In a world struggling increasingly with mental illness, our disconnection from the natural world is likely a significant contributing factor. In the late 20th century, R.S. Urlich researched the impact of the natural world on human psychology. His research demonstrated that people who saw urban scenes tended to feel sadness, aggression, and anger while those who saw scenes of nature felt increases in positive feelings such as affection, joy, friendliness, and playfulness. The data demonstrated that when adults saw landscapes of nature, they experienced an increased production of serotonin, the key hormone for stabilizing our mood, and increasing feelings of well-being and happiness. Urlich's research went on to show that patients recovered more quickly from surgery if they had a window that enabled them to see nature as opposed to views of walls or concrete from their hospital beds.[52]

Dr. Jason Strauss, director of geriatric psychiatry at Harvard-affiliated Cambridge Health Alliance says that for people who experience mood disorders "interacting with nature is one of the best self-improvement tools they can use."[53]

> **MEDITATION #4**
> **REFLECTION ON TIME SPENT IN NATURE**

1) Choose a quiet outdoor location which includes an object in nature which you consider to be beautiful - trees, flowers, water, a mountainous view, or even something more simple like a rock, a branch, or a leaf.

2) Think about a current issue or challenge in your life which causes you stress, anxiety, or anger.

3) Give a number to your stress level - 1 being the lowest and 10 being the highest.

4) Be in a position that allows your muscles to relax and turn your eyes to the beautiful object you chose.

5) While staring at the object, begin to take simple breaths. Notice as you inhale and exhale at a slow, consistent pace for a few minutes.

6) Think about the object you are looking at. Ask yourself: Where did it come from? How did it become what it is now? What about the object stands out to you? Does the object bring up any memories for you? Is there something that you wonder about the object? Spend a few minutes reflecting on the object and these questions.

7) Spend a few minutes focusing on your breath.

8) Think about the topic that brings you stress again. Give a number to your stress level now, from 1-10.

9) Take a few minutes to journal about the experience and how your connection to nature impacted your stress and anxiety

10) Take a moment to reflect on the gratitude you feel toward nature for this experience

Please see APPENDIX B on page 161 for modern day nature-related therapies.

STEWARDS OF NATURE

The benefits of spending time in nature in terms of our physical, emotional and spiritual health are numerous.

There is one catch.

We cannot benefit from what does not exist. Our natural world is precious. We are part of it and it is part of us. And when we carelessly and needlessly destroy, however quickly or slowly, the very resources on which we depend for our physical, mental, and spiritual health, we will feel that lack keenly. It is only a matter of time. We are so fortunate to be living in a world so rich in natural resources and to have the privilege of benefitting from them. But with privilege comes responsibility and we must do our part in caring for it.

Genesis teaches that "The Lord God took the Man and put him in the Garden of Eden to work it and take care of it." (2:15) Ancient Jewish tradition teaches that "When God created Adam, He took him and showed him all of creation and said to Adam, 'See my works, how fine and excellent they are. All that I have created I created for you. Think about this and do not ruin and destroy My world.'"[54]

Protecting the environment from needless destruction has long been part of Jewish ritual tradition which works in perfect consonance with the modern-day recognition of the importance of conservation, recycling, and a shift to clean, renewable energies. As Samson Raphael Hirsch taught in the mid-19th century: *"The earth was not created as a gift to you. You have been given to the earth, to treat it with respectful consideration as God's earth, and everything on it must be seen as God's creation…to be respected, loved, and helped to attain their purpose according to God's will."*[55]

The Bible teaches that 48 cities were to be established in Israel for the tribe of Levi which was designated to serve as the spiritual guides for the nation. (Moses came from this tribe.) The Bible stipulates that each of these cities must have 1,000 cubits (approximately 2,500 feet) of "open space" in all directions around each of the cities, outside its built up and industrial areas.

(Numbers 35:2-5). Scholars in the Talmud taught that the city inhabitants were allowed to plant flowers and trees in this space but nothing else. They also explained that the rest of the nation was expected to follow these leaders and establish "Green Belts" around all the cities in Israel.[56] Rabbi Shlomo Yitzchaki [known as "Rashi"], a medieval French winemaker who is one of the premiere Biblical commentators, teaches that the purpose of this space was for the city inhabitants to have aesthetic beauty to enjoy. Ovadia ben Jacob Sforno, an early 16th century Italian Biblical commentator, philosopher, and physician, explains that this was a space where people could "cultivate beehives or raise doves." The message is clear. The city dwellers were to have a place where they could exalt in the beauty of God's creations, and in which they could commune with nature - activities which could bring them relaxation from the hustle and bustle of city life while also rejuvenating their spirits.

Thus, over 3,500 years ago God's biblical instructions's biblical instructions guided man regarding the critical role which the open and beautiful outdoors must play if we seek to focus on soul work in our lives. The scholars in the Talmudic era, 2,000 years ago, took this to heart and taught that one must strive to live in a city that includes a garden.[57]

You have been gifted with a precious gem, one that can help you achieve greater spiritual, emotional, and mental health. It's called nature. And it's right outside your door. Find the aspect of nature that speaks to you and your soul, and then make sure to go and enjoy it!

CHAPTER SEVEN

MUSIC AND SOUL

We sat in a circle, eyes closed. All was dark except for the glow of the small candle burning on the desk in the middle of the room.

Our teacher began to sing, "Yai dai dai dai dai dai." Slowly, but surely, the group of students picked up the tune. At first, I felt a bit uncomfortable. I let out a small giggle intended for my friend sitting next to me. After some muffled laughter, we both silently decided to concentrate on the singing.

I closed my eyes more tightly and listened. The music became more familiar, the repetition of the melody got stuck in my head. I knew where the song was headed next. I anticipated the low notes at the beginning and the high notes in the middle. Soon, no one was there but the music and me. I felt carried away by the song. I heard my voice alone. Then I heard it surrounded by everyone else. We were in unison. Individual voices sang the same melody. No real words backed up our song. There were no words that could. I wanted to sing forever.

It was over too soon. We opened our eyes. No one said anything.

"How do you feel?" she asked.

"I feel relaxed," said one student.

"Everything feels more in focus," said another.

Our teacher smiled. She told us the song was called a niggun. A niggun, she continued, is a song without words. It was a powerful form of Jewish meditation.

In song, our individual experiences get expressed in a unified way. We understand that the song that is the human experience connects us even when our stories may be somewhat different.... When we listen to music, we connect to something beyond ourselves. We feel united with other human beings and to our deepest selves as souls. Judaism teaches that the mouth, the instrument of our bodies, connects the heart with the soul. When we join body with soul, we are complete. The music creates a state where we are in tune with our essential spiritual selves and can feel united with our Creator.[58]

"*If I were not a physicist I would probably be a musician. I often think in music. I live my daydreams in music. I see my life in terms of music.*" - Albert Einstein[59]

THE ANCIENT POWER OF MUSIC

It's the earliest years of civilization. Genesis. The very beginning of the Bible relates that humans were first learning how to make all the basic necessities for life - building tents, understanding how to breed animals, and creating tools and vessels (Genesis 4:20, 22). Mixed in among these obvious human needs we find that they also invented "the harp and the flute." (Genesis 4:21) What are those doing there?

It is clear that early civilizations knew intuitively that life was not just about food and shelter. They understood that they also had to tend to their spiritual side, to their souls, and that music was an essential part of that effort.

Fast forward five Biblical books to the end of Deuteronomy. Moses shares his last will and testament with the nation of Israel on the last day of his life. And he chooses to sing a song that foretells their long and often painful future as a nation, with a message of hope that clarity, peace, and redemption will come at the end of the story. Why did Moses choose to share this message in a song?

Moses clearly understood that like warm water dissolves sugar, song softens the message so it more easily enters our hearts. He also knew that musical messages stay with us more readily than simply spoken words because they penetrate right to the soul. Think about how many songs you know the lyrics to compared to speeches you have heard that you know by heart! This is because they are not simply pieces of information stored in your brain but they contain messages that connect and lodge within your soul.

Diane Austin, adjunct professor of music therapy at New York University and executive director of the Music Psychotherapy Center in New York teaches that *"Nothing accesses the inner world of feelings, sensations, memories, and associations as directly as music does."*

Dr. Anne Fabiny, Editor in Chief of Harvard Women's Health Watch explains that *"Listening to and performing music reactivates areas of the brain associated with memory, reasoning, speech, emotion, and reward. Two recent studies—one in the United States and the other in Japan—found that music doesn't just help us retrieve stored memories, it also helps us lay down new ones.*[60]

The Bible relates that the prophet Elisha said, "Now bring me a musician" and then records that God appeared to Elisha. He needed to connect to his soul to experience prophecy and music enabled him to do so. (Kings II 3:15) The theme of prophets using music to connect spiritually and achieve Divine prophecy is repeated often in the Bible. (See Samuel I 10:5 and Chronicles I 25:1 for examples of this)

This is why music and song can be found in connection with the ritual services of so many faiths - organs and choirs in Chirstian churches, the "adhan" musical call to prayer from Islamic mosques, the orchestra and songs of the Levites in the Jewish Temple, the "kirtan" singing and "ragis" musicians in Sikh and Hindu Temples, and the chants and musical instruments involved in many Buddhist practices.

It is worth noting that the numerical value of the Hebrew word for song, "Shira," is 515 - the same numerical value as the Hebrew word for prayer, "Tefila." Song and prayer have a similar capacity to facilitate our connection with our souls and Creator. Going one step deeper, song is a form of prayer, as demonstrated by King David, who you will read about shortly.

[Dov] *The spiritual power of music never ceases to amaze me. When I am the cantor in the synagogue, and the congregation sings the prayers along with me, I feel the energy of the song rise up around me, lifting me beyond the physical limitations of this world and into another realm. A realm where I can leave the challenges of this world behind, feel the embrace of the Divine, and experience happiness, peace, and calm. I wish I could bottle those moments up so I can feel them all the time.*

In general music helps me reorient myself to where I want to be emotionally and spiritually. When I am feeling emotionally down, fast paced, high energy music helps me tap into the inner happiness which always rests inside, waiting to burst free. When I feel spiritually disconnected, slow, soulful songs with either harmonious instrumentals or meaningful Biblical words help me reconnect.

Music also connects me spiritually in other ways. My great-grandfather was a rabbi, author, and composer who lived in Hungary. He was murdered by the Nazis in the gas chamber of Auschwitz but his songs remain. Four of his children miraculously survived the hell of the Holocaust and every Friday night, as we begin our Sabbath meal, scores of his descendants ranging from grandchildren to great-great-great-grandchildren, sing the tune he composed as we welcome the Sabbath angels into our homes. When I close my eyes and sing his tune, I can visualize this man who I never met or even saw in a picture. Through my great-grandfather's song, I can literally feel his presence and connect to him deeply.

MUSIC AS A SPIRITUAL BRIDGE

Rabbi Judah Loew, a 16th century biblical scholar and philosopher (also known as "the Maharal") teaches that since the world was created in seven days, the number seven symbolizes the physical world. It also connotes the limitations of the physical world which came into being during the seven days of Creation. The Maharal continues by saying the next number we count, eight, represents the level above and beyond nature. Eight lifts us up and out of the material world and into the supernatural or spiritual realm. It is in this realm that we have greater access to our spiritual essence and the gravity of our physical selves lessens.[61] Interestingly, the symbol for infinity is an eight lying on its side.

Rabbi Loew teaches that this is why the Jewish holiday of Hannukah lasts for eight days. The eight symbolizes the miraculous nature of that period of time, with the last day of the holiday being a particularly powerful time to access the highest realms of spirituality through prayer and reflection.

"Kaballah," ancient Jewish mysticism, explains that this why musical scales are divided into eight notes called "octaves:" C, D, E, F, G, A, B, C or do, re, mi, fa, sol, la, tee, do. The eight notes in the octaves indicate the spiritual nature of music and its ability to transport us into the spiritual realm.

Going a bit deeper into the musical scales, the C or "do" which begins and ends each octave is made up of 440 vibrations. In Hebrew, each letter is equal to a numerical value. The first letter "aleph" equals one, the second letter "bet" equals two, until it reaches ten. After 10, each subsequent letter jumps by ten until it reaches 100. After 100, each subsequent letter jumps by another 100, The letter that equals 400 is the last letter in the alphabet - "tuf." The letter that equals 40, right in the middle of the alphabet, is "mem." You add those two letters together to equal 440 and when you spell them together it spells "tam" which means "completion." No human has even been or will ever be perfect. But we do strive to be as whole and integrated as possible. According to Kabalistic sources, the notes of the musical scale are a vehicle for this internal integration as music's evocative nature allows us to connect with our soul and soul purpose.

> *Music cuts through the protective shell of our psyche, piercing our consciousness, and allowing access to the soft, inner seed inside from which new life can grow.*
>
> *Music is the language of the soul. It cuts through the protective shell of our psyche, pierces our consciousness, and allows access to the inner seed where new life can grow.*

In the succinct and powerful words of musician and composer Dan Martinez:

"Music is the language of the soul. When you hear it, you recognize that it is familiar, something you like, and has your attention. Better than conversation with a friend, it lets you talk and think what you want, remember memories, allows you to come along for a ride, and stay for as long as you want."[62]

CELESTIAL MUSIC

The scientific and astrological world also throw their weight behind the connection between music and spirituality. Astrology, the Zodiac, and horoscopes - disciplines that have been studied and accepted in societies for thousands of years - all attribute spiritual power to the alignment of the planets and stars. Biblical sources understand that these celestial objects produce sound waves which convey the spiritual influence that they have on the universe as translated via astrology. The Zohar, a mystical work which goes back 2,000 years, and Maimonides from the 12th century, both teach that the sound waves that emanate from the stars and constellations actually create music. [63] Moshe Chaim Luzatto, the 18th century philosopher and mystic who we quoted extensively regarding our souls, takes this one step further, bringing out the commutative property of music and the constellations when he says that: "All the luminaries (the planets)...are motivated by music."[64]

Space probes such as Voyager and Galileo gather and transmit sounds that emanate from celestial bodies and send them back to Earth. Scientists then process the data so we can actually hear those sounds. As scientists have discovered, just as each person's voice is unique, each planet emits its own "song".[65]

Kabbalah teaches that the letters of the Hebrew word for playing music, "nagen," demonstrate the power of music to connect body to soul. "Nagen" is made up of three Hebrew letters - "nun," gimmel," and "nun." According to Kabbalah, this acronym represents the e three parts of a human that come alive through actively engaging with music - our very life force ("nefesh" which starts with a "nun"), our bodies ("guf which starts with a "gimmel") and our souls ("neshama" which starts with a "nun").

This connection to music is actually part of our spiritual DNA. The Midrash, a compilation of ancient Jewish teachings, explains that song pacifies and soothes a baby because it brings a baby back to the spiritual existence from which it recently came. It reconnects the baby to its soul and the soul world, bringing comfort to a child that has suddenly appeared in the physical world. [66]

MUSIC AS A UNIFIER

Rabbi Gedaliah Schorr, a 20th century American Biblical and Talmudic scholar, draws inspiration from another aspect of music. Like various instruments all playing their own score, the universe often seems disjointed and chaotic. But a master conductor can take those seemingly disparate elements and bring them together in harmonious cooperation. When we align our inner world with this universal spiritual reality, it gives us a sense of peace, calm and happiness. Music helps us do that. Rabbi Schorr relates this idea to Moses' song about his nation's history referenced at the beginning of this chapter. It brings together the seemingly unconnected past, present and future and shows how they all come together as part of God's plan. All three dimensions are revealed to the prophet as a total reality in which there is no conflict, and in which future and past events are not only in harmony, but clarify one another. Thus, everything is melded as if it were all happening at the same time. The most effective mechanism to convey that message is song, which gives tangible expression to that which is disjointed, coming together in harmony.[67]

There is another powerful spiritual role music can play in our lives that speaks to the core of our humanity. Human beings have a fundamental need to feel seen and understood. Without that, we feel alone in the most painful way. Music can help with that existential loneliness. When a song expresses what you are feeling, when it says what you want to say or moves you in a way you want to be moved, it opens you up and allows you to connect more deeply to your own soul. It also promotes a sense of common humanity, of being understood and accompanied by others on your life journey. That sense of shared destiny is a powerful salve for even the most challenging times in our lives.

[**Atara**] *It's hard for me to even articulate the breadth and depth of the value of music to me. It's my friend and constant companion, my alter ego, my words when I can't find them, my partner in crime. It's my tears when I can't cry them, my anger when I need to release it, and my movie reel fantasy when I need to escape. It is the arms wrapped around me, shot of adrenaline, imagination gone wild or soothing voice I need at any given moment. It's all the sides of me.*

THE LANGUAGE OF KING DAVID

King David was a warrior and a musician - he lived with fiery passion. He also faced significant internal and external battles throughout his 70-year lifetime. With every challenge that King David confronted, he turned to music to help him process and express his innermost feelings, get clarity on what he most wanted and needed for himself and from God, and to reconnect with his truest self - his soul.

David observed the transformative power of music at a young age when King Saul, his predecessor, called upon the young boy to play the harp for him when the king felt deep sadness. As the Bible records, *"And it happened that whenever the spirit of melancholy from God was upon Saul, David would take the harp and play it with his hand, and Saul would feel relieved and it would be well with him, and the spirit of melancholy would depart from him."* (Samuel I 16:23)

This lesson served King David well throughout his life - one often punctured by strife, sadness, and struggles. When King David wrote "The days of our years among them are seventy years, and for the mighty eighty years. And most of them are filled with toil and pain" (90:10), he was speaking autobiographically.

A mere shepherd boy, he was anointed to be King of Israel with no choice in the matter, while his seven older brothers watched in jealousy. It took 15 years for him to be accepted as king, while the incumbent King Saul pursued him to kill him. King Saul also forced a separation between David and his closest and dearest friend, Saul's son, Jonathan. David finally becomes king of all Israel but his reign is replete with wars, rebellions and assassination attempts - even from his own son Absalom! - family and marriage dysfunction, children going astray, scandals including a sexual encounter with Batsheva, another man's wife, which led to a punishment of the death of his son, and seemingly not a moment of physical calm and physical peace.

These difficulties are recorded in the Book of Samuel. We can learn how he dealt with these challenges through his own words in the Book of Psalms. Better put, through his own *songs* in Psalms.

King David began many of his Psalms with the Hebrew word "*Laminatzeach*" which means "to the conductor," giving musical instruction to the person leading the music in his song. David not only sang but played his lyre while singing his way through life. He ends the entire book of Psalms by singing:

"Praise Him with lyre and harp. Praise Him with drum and dance. Praise Him with organ and flute. Praise Him with clanging cymbals. Praise Him with resonant trumpets." And then he adds that playing these instruments enabled the expression of "the entire soul."

King David used music to connect to his soul, truly understand what he was feeling, and to express it.

Music served as the primary vehicle for David to articulate his feelings and to be fully present with his emotional reality. He sings, ""How great is my suffering." (3:2) He is very aware of what he is experiencing. David records that "every night I drench my bed with tears." (6:8) David sings openly about the anger that he feels, for example: "My eyes are dimmed from anger." (6:9) He also relates his fears: "My soul is utterly terrified." (6:4)

He sings about not taking destructive action based on those negative emotions: "Be angry, but do not sin. Speak in your heart upon your bed and remain silent." (4:5) David is literally telling himself - through song - not to act on his anger but, rather, to work it through as he goes to sleep and to proactively allow it to simmer down.

Whereas most people experiencing sadness and anger, and whose lives are filled with conflict have a difficult time sleeping, King David declares, in song, that "in peace, in harmony, I lie down and sleep." (4:9)

David does not shy away from revealing how he accomplished that. The entire Book of Psalms gives it away. He played his instrument and sang at all times in his life - both the good and the bad. David begins his songs with words such as "As he fled from Absalom his son" (chapter 3). "Upon the death of Labben" (Chapter 9). "A song for the inauguration of the Temple" (Chapter 30) "When he disguised himself as insane before Abimelech" (Chapter 34). "When Nathan the prophet came to him when he slept with Batsheva" (Chapter 51). His music enabled him to live with self-awareness at all times and to remain even keeled and focused even in the face of strong emotions.

There is a deeper message to the word "*Laminatzeiach*", "to the conductor," with which King David opened so many of his songs. The idea that this word also carries the meaning of "victory" is commonly attributed to Rabbi Elijah Ben Solomon, an 18th-century biblical and Talmudic scholar known as "the Vilna Gaon." According to this interpretation, King David was declaring "to victory" as he began playing his music, knowing that music would enable him to reach deep inside and help him defeat his own internal fear and negativity—emotions a king can ill afford to fall prey to.

EXERCISE #6: YOUR DAILY "INTENTION MUSIC" PLAYLIST

1. Pick an area of your life that you would like to work on. Think about 4 things:
   a) Where are you now?
   b) Where do you want to go?
   c) What do you need to get there? For example - support, financial resources, space, clarity)
   d) What are your primary obstacles to getting there? For example - time, peer pressure, resource constraints, limiting beliefs about yourself, fear)
2. We strongly recommend writing these down to have in front of you as you go through this exercise. ,
3. Imagine how what you want for yourself looks like. Really feel it. Then choose a song or two that represent that feeling or achievement for you.
4. Think more about the things you listed that you need to get to that goal. What songs represent that?-
5. Reflect upon the potential obstacles that you wrote down. What do they sound like in song? What songs represent you navigating around or blowing up those obstacles?
6. Is there a song that represents the image in your mind of a totally clear road in front of you leading to your goal?

7. Keep your new playlist handy. Set aside a quiet time in your daily schedule to review what you wrote about what you want to achieve and play the songs you chose as you reflect on the various steps. Play the song or songs that you chose for whatever aspect comes to you - the goal, what you need to get there, or the obstacles. Listen to the song on repeat a couple of times. Feel the music deeply. Let it penetrate and move you. Then, as it continues to play, ask yourself what you need today to take another positive step in the direction you want to go. Do you need strength? Do you need calm? Do you need inner power? Do you need energy? Do you need a clearer path? Do you need peaceful open space?

8. If you repeat this exercise daily, and those songs or new songs that you choose become part of your daily routine, you will likely find yourself empowered to take the bold steps you need to take to achieve what previously seemed to be unattainable goals.

Music has an almost magical quality to transmute our moods and our state of mind. It can carry our biggest emotions, soften our roughest edges, expose our rawest feelings, and raise our inner vibration to be more consonant with our soul.

In the words of Plato, "Music is the movement of sound to reach the soul for the education of its virtue."

HOW TO SOUL

CHAPTER EIGHT

MOVEMENT AND SOUL

Estee Schwab, a mother of many children, who works as an Executive function/ADHD specialist relates: "My predawn movement time is focused on myself and my Creator. It is my time to connect, to think, and to live. It is my time to be authentically and passionately me. Movement links my mind, body and soul. Movement relaxes me, creating endless space for personal creativity and spirituality."

Estee's 17-year-old son, Menachem, echoes his mother's feelings: "I love running because it is a healthy way to let out my energy which helps me focus and enables me to be more productive in my religious studies. Running helps me find my true self by making me a happier person which enhances my relationship with God. I look forward all day to the awesome feeling I get during my run; there is simply nothing like it!"

WE ARE DESIGNED TO MOVE

What is a chapter about exercise and movement doing in a book about soul and spiritual connection to ourselves and our creator?

The soul is housed in a body. The mind is connected to the body and interprets what the body is experiencing. Emotions are run through the body. As long as the soul is in the body, they work as a unit, even if they are different in essence. To ignore one is to the detriment of the other - we need to nurture both. How do we know what the body needs to support the spiritual work we are here to do?

We can look at the design of the body for the answer. Humans are made to move. Our bodies are designed to walk, run, jump, twist, bend, reach, squat, push, and pull. If our optimal function was sitting, our 206 bones, 360 joints, 900 ligaments, and 4,000 tendons would be unnecessary.

For most of world history, we didn't have to make a conscious decision to exercise. Movement was built into life. We went to the river to hand wash our clothes, we chopped wood for fuel, we worked the land for food, we walked almost everywhere, and our sleep was synched with the rising and setting of the sun. In the past, being active was called "life."

Today, we sit for work, we drive for transportation, we have machines that wash our clothing and dishes, and our most popular entertainment is watching something on a screen. So now we have to intentionally incorporate movement into our lives. Now it's called "exercise." Because the modern lifestyle is so sedentary, if we want to be healthy, we have to make a conscious and consistent effort to be active. We have to work to keep our bodies moving - doing what they are designed to do.

When physical activity is part of our daily life, the body hums like a well oiled machine. Energy levels go up, moods lift, confidence increases and our spirits open. Without regular exercise, without getting our blood pumping, our physical and mental reservoirs turn gunky and the mechanisms struggle to run smoothly. Our immune systems downshift, our natural endorphins decrease and stress hormones run amok.

THE BODY-SOUL CONNECTION

Volumes have been written about this mind-body connection (a moniker that makes a somewhat artificial distinction between intertwined aspects of our physical selves). But does this have anything to do with our soul? The mind and body are physical. We can touch them, see them, examine them, alter them. But the soul is not physical. So is it impacted by how we treat our bodies? Does the soul "care" if we exercise or not?

The Bible teaches, "Protect yourselves very carefully." [Deuteronomy 4:15] The Talmudic Sages understood this to mean that a person must live a healthy lifestyle and take care of the body.[68] Why would the Bible, which serves as a spiritual guide, not only issue a command about care for the physical body but use the extra language urging us to be very careful about this?

On the most basic level, while it's true that the soul is not physical, there is a direct relationship between our body and soul.

The body is the home of the soul and the vehicle by which the soul expresses itself in this world. When the body is experiencing pain, discomfort or disease, it limits our bandwidth for spiritual pursuits.

It is hard to focus on prayer, doing for others and self-actualization when the body is in need of attention. By extension, healthy spiritual practices can help to heal the body when it's in distress. Belief in a spiritual reality and a meaningful existence can help us get through illness and tough times. Moving our bodies to whatever extent possible helps with both.

Let's see what that looks like in real time.

[Atara] *One of the most fulfilling and pleasurable experiences of my life (albeit a 24-7 job) was owning a women's wellness studio for four years. My partner and I named the studio "The Tribe" before that moniker was even a 'thing' because it was a play on words for us. It was a reference to our target market - the female religious Jewish community (think biblical 12 Tribes). It was also a reference to a new type of community that we wanted to build. What did that new community look like?*

When I became religiously observant in the late 1990's, I noticed that many of the lifestyle habits that brought me joy and kept me feeling healthy and balanced were not common in the religious community. These habits included healthy and moderate eating, physical exercise, athletics, and an appreciation for nature. I used to joke that when I would go out for a run, people would look behind me to see who was chasing me! There was also a lack of education about the importance of healthy living and caring for the body. The reasons for these omissions in healthy lifestyle practices have both practical and cultural roots but I knew that the Bible supports care of the body as a home for the soul. So I set out to change all that. I wanted people to know that not only could they balance their religious lifestyle with healthy living but that the two go hand in hand. And so we opened The Tribe.

The Tribe offered fitness classes of all kinds, personal and small group training, and training for running and Spartan events. We also hosted workshops on a range of wellness topics including nutrition, mindfulness, life balance, body image, and integrative hormonal health. As time went on, we watched the women get fit and feel great from the inside out.

As it grew, The Tribe became known as a space of positive energy, creativity, and learning. It was also a place of acceptance - all deeply spiritual values. Orthodox Judaism places emphasis on more subdued behavior and modest dress which covers most of the body when one is in the public sphere. As a result, the women lacked a space where they could literally (many cover their hair in public) and figuratively let their hair down. At The Tribe, women knew they were entering a zone of no judgment, no requirements. Just show up and do your thing.

Unlike many fitness studios, the ethos at the studio was never about the aesthetic of exercise. My instructors would never tell you to work harder to fit into skinny jeans or look better in a bikini (though that's fine if it motivates you to move!). Rather, we were all about what feeling strong, fit, and comfortable in your own body does for your spirit, your energy, your confidence, and how you move through the world. We preached the art of balancing challenging your body with listening to your body. And that doing something hard might be uncomfortable but it's not bad - in the studio and in life. In other words, the Tribe was a soul-based fitness studio. If what you brought to the fitness floor and what you took home with you didn't make you better in some small way, it wasn't worth doing.

To that end, we also had inspirational quotes all over the walls. My personal favorite was "Most people will go their whole lives and never know how good this feels."

It reflected what I saw over and over again and what I heard from Tribe clients even today, many years after closing our doors. When your body is strong, supple, and healthy, and your mind is calm and clear, you can literally take on the world. When your body is burdened by a lack of self care, it drags you down physically, emotionally, and spiritually. You feel self-conscious, low energy, and low confidence. You simply can't be all you can be in a body that feels ill at ease.

Most people know that if we neglect movement and don't make an effort to exercise, it puts us at risk for every modern disease we know of: diabetes, cancer, autoimmune disease, Alzheimer's disease, heart disease, obesity, arthritis, and the list goes on. Bookshelves and online resources list titles by the thousands about the connection between exercise and physical health. But what we must also recognize is that we pay a high price emotionally and spiritually for our inactive lifestyle.

In the 12th century, physician and sage Maimonides taught that *"Whoever is idle and does not exercise...even if he eats the proper foods and takes care to follow the rules of medicine, will be full of pain for all his days and his strength will fade away."*[69]

When we are sedentary, the hinges get rusty and cobwebs grow in the corners of our bodies and minds. We feel murky, sluggish, stiff, and unwell. Depression and anxiety also take root more easily in this untended physical environment.

Dax Shepard, actor and Armchair Expert podcaster, who interviews celebrities, journalists, and academics about their lives, was interviewed by professor, author and podcaster Brene Brown in her *Unlocking Us* podcast.[70] Shepard, who has struggled with substance abuse, was asked by Brown what is something he does regularly, a practice or a habit, that's hard as [anything] but totally worth it.

"Definitely exercise. Exercise is the most important cornerstone to me not feeling miserable and discontent... If I had to give up all the tools I have, I think that would be the last one I give up. That seems to have the most effect on my mental attitude."

THE HEALING IMPACT OF MOVEMENT

Brown then asks if exercise is a pillar of Shepard's sobriety. Shepard's answer? "1000%." Shepard answers by discussing his approach when a guy he's sponsoring (in a twelve-step program) calls him up to complain about something upsetting. Shepard lets him know that he is more than happy to listen but first he tells the guy to "take a one hour walk or go to the gym for an hour" and then to call Shepard back and he'll listen to everything the guy wants to say. "Almost 100% of the time that concern they had has gone down [in intensity] by 80%. I just haven't had the experience where they've done that and then called me back and they are still as crazy in their head about the thing."

In the same episode, Brown asks the identical question to Tim Ferriss, an American entrepreneur, investor, author, podcaster, and one of Fortune's "40 under 40". Ferriss answers the question by saying, "I also just want to second what Dax said that if someone put a gun against my head and said you have to choose one of all these tools in the tool kit for sort of mental and emotional stability and resilience, I would also choose exercise. Easily. Not even a close second place."

From a macro view, the body and soul are distinctive yet intertwined. The body is physical, the soul is not. Neither can change the absolute essence of the other. But the state of one directly impacts the potential of the other. You can't do all that you are meant to do in this world if you don't have your health or your sanity. Conversely, focusing on the body alone is "vanity of vanities" as King Solomon states repeatedly in Ecclesiastes. It's missing the deeper meaning of life - the part of life that you *can* take with you when your physical existence comes to an end. In other words, it's the combination of caring for the body and feeding the soul that forms the DNA - the double helix - of a life fully lived.

Entrepreneur and author Mike Schiemer describes his life-saving journey with self-care in a 2012 interview with Shape.com. *"I've always struggled greatly with low self-esteem, clinical depression, mood disorder, and severe anxiety, as well as alcoholism in the past. These have been exacerbated by working too much, putting too much pressure on myself, not taking care of my health and fitness, along with other external stressors. I became so stressed out, depressed, and chemically imbalanced that I was incapacitated and couldn't get through normal daily activities... I nearly committed suicide before turning myself over to the emergency room last minute."*[71]

When professional medical help didn't give Mike the relief he needed he explored lifestyle changes. *"I had to slowly start out walking one to two miles and after many months, I eventually progressed to running four to six miles. This helped to boost my natural endorphin production, which in turn helped my mood."* Next, Mike added weightlifting, meditation, and breathing exercises to his routine. Eventually, he says, the exercise *"helped save my life by naturally reducing stress, improving my breathing abilities and patterns, helped me slow down my breathing, balance my body's chemicals, clear my head, give me more energy, improve self-esteem, and return my testosterone levels to normal healthy levels."*

Here is the simple and undeniable truth: our bodies need to move. Our minds need our bodies to move. *And our souls need our bodies to move.*

[Dov] *I have gone through ups and downs in terms of commitment to regular physical activity. Weight control has always been a challenge for me in my adult years and my motivator for exercise was always related to keeping my weight under control. But I can see a direct correlation between how much better I feel overall when I am in a mode of daily exercise and how that positively impacts my ability to connect spiritually, especially with regard to prayer.*

THE GREATEST MEDICINE

Abraham Isaac Kook wrote that physical movement enables the body to "illuminate" the soul and that exercise "strengthens one's spiritual light." [72] Around the same time, Rabbi Israel Meir Kagan, a leading spiritual mentor in early 20th century Poland, taught his students that they must exercise and break a sweat on a daily basis or they will not succeed in their studies and their spiritual pursuits.[73]

These sources, and life experience, seem to indicate an even deeper connection between movement and our spirituality. How does exercise help us connect with our souls?

Like tension on a rubber band, the body is designed to handle some physical and emotional stress and retain its elasticity. In small doses, "stress hormones" including cortisol, adrenaline and epinephrine, can heighten memory, increase immune system function, and lower sensitivity to pain. But when stress is too much for too long, like the rubber band under too much tension, it reduces our tensile strength. High and constant levels of cortisol lower immunity, raise blood pressure, inhibit insulin production, raise blood sugar, impact sleep, and wreak havoc on our mental and emotional state.

Enter stage left - exercise - arguably the greatest medicine known to humankind. Exercise is a double dose of protection from the negative impacts of long term stress. It literally burns off the stress hormones and replaces them with powerful endorphins like serotonin and dopamine that give us a deep sense of wellbeing and a feeling of connection to ourselves and to others. It quiets the loud buzzing in our minds and bodies that block out softer sounds like that of the soul. Exercise also softens and opens our minds so we can think more clearly and creatively, allowing us to think in terms of possibilities rather than survival. Instead of just grinding through the day, exercise helps us make the shift to a decidedly more spiritual state of higher consciousness and possibility.

> *Exercise quiets the loud buzzing in our minds and bodies that block out softer sounds like that of the soul*

TIME TO MOVE

On a practical level, you might be wondering how to incorporate exercise into your (already too busy) daily life? Or what kind of exercise is best? And how often and for how long do you need to exercise to reap the physical and mental benefits?

How you choose to move is an individual decision. There is no one-size-fits-all. It could be hiking, running, swimming, walking, dancing, strength training, yoga, cycling, skiing, tennis, basketball or, ideally, a combination of different forms of movement. *What* you do is less critical than *how often* you do it and that you spend some of your exercise time (safely) out of your physical comfort zone.

It's also important that you choose forms of exercise that you enjoy. If you hate your exercise routine, you are unlikely to stick to it, even with the best intentions. Keep in mind that aside from personal preference, other factors that may impact your choice of exercise include location and season or climate, access to fitness facilities and the outdoors, goals, body type, budget, space, and time. The minimum recommended weekly exercise time is 150 minutes of moderate-intensity exercise per week. That time can be broken up into intervals of exercise as short as 5-10 minutes if that's what works best for your schedule.

Please see APPENDIX C on page 163 for additional information and data about the connection between physical activity and mental/physical health

There is another notable parallel between self-care and spiritual growth. Figuring out what works best for your body mirrors the process of connecting with your soul. You have to hold outside noise at an arm's length - media, what works for other people, pressures, and expectations - and really tune in to what makes your body feel alive, nurtured, vibrant, whole, and healthy.

EXERCISE #7: EXERCISE AS A SPIRITUAL PRACTICE

There are several pathways for creating a spiritual practice through exercise: focus, gratitude, and mind body connection. Each is explained below. Choose one to help you connect spiritually when you exercise. Of course, you can rotate from one to another.

Focus: When you're engaging in physical activity, it brings you into the present moment and allows for greater mindfulness and presence. This can help you achieve a meditative state and clear your thoughts, allowing you to connect with your soul on a deeper level.

Before your next exercise session, jot down your answers to the following questions:

1. What is your mind chatter about right now?
2. Are the thoughts focused on the past or the future?
3. What adjective/s best describe what you are feeling right now? (could be physically, emotionally, mentally, or spiritually - whatever feels dominant at the moment)

4. If someone told you right now to pause and drop into a meditative state, how doable does that feel?

After your exercise session, repeat the above questions and jot them down as well. How did your answers differ before and after physical activity?

Gratitude: Exercise can be a way to express and experience gratitude for the gift of a healthy body and the ability to move. By taking care of your physical health, you can show gratitude for the blessings in your life and strengthen your spiritual connection.

After an exercise session:
1. Create a gratitude list for all that had to be working well for you to exercise today: i.e. your heart pumps blood; your muscles, ligaments and tendons are strong and agile, your eyes see, the nerves in your skin function, allowing you to feel the sun or the cool air or the breeze, etc., your lungs take in oxygen and expand and contract well with your breath, etc.
2. Imagine if even one of the functions on your body gratitude list isn't working. How would that change your ability to do what you did today for exercise?
3. Take a moment to breathe and experience how that gratitude feels in your body. What does that open up for you?

Mind-body-soul connection: Exercise can help you develop a greater awareness of your body and the sensations you're experiencing. This heightened awareness can be a gateway to spiritual insights and a deeper understanding of your place in the world.

Before and after your next exercise session, jot down your answers to the following in your journal. The scale is 1-5 with the lower numbers reflecting a more positive state of being.

1. What is your stress level? (1 not stressed at all; 5 very stressed)
2. Physical comfort or discomfort (1 very comfortable; 5 very uncomfortable)
3. What is your energy level? (1 very high energy; 5 very low energy)

4. What is your mood like? (1 very good mood; 5 very low mood)
5. What sensations do you notice in your body?
6. What other healthy choices does a regular exercise routine inspire you to make in your life?

When it comes to exercise and soul, the goal is to create an exercise *practice* or *habit* - similar to going to the grocery store or brushing your teeth or calling your mother on Sundays. To stick with exercise long enough to become a habit, you have to choose forms of movement that you can and *want to* incorporate into your daily life. If you've chosen the right forms of exercise for your body and soul, you will feel energized, alive, centered and ready to take on the world at the end of a workout or activity. If you feel drained, shamed, or adverse to doing that activity again, try a different form of movement. There are literally endless ways to move your body to boost your mind and spirit. It's just a matter of experimenting to find the one that's right for you - physically and spiritually.

HOW TO SOUL

CHAPTER NINE

FOOD AND SOUL

OUR DEEP CONNECTION TO FOOD

[**Atara**] *I recently started working with a client, Jennifer, in her mid-50's who is a self-defined sugar and junk food addict. In our initial coaching session, I asked her when and how the "addiction" started. She said from a very young age she remembers trading her school lunch for junk food and spending pocket change on sugary snacks. When I asked if there was a particular trigger for that behavior, she said she grew up in a home where there was little affection or warmth so she leaned into pleasure foods to comfort herself and fill the emotional void. There was also little spirituality in the home. In her youth she was active so while she was never thin, she was able to manage her weight to a greater or lesser degree. But the behavior of turning to food to fill a void in her life soon turned into a deeply ingrained habit.*

Fast forward several decades. Jennifer is blessed with a loving husband, many children, and a close-knit community. At the same time, she struggles with obesity, low self-esteem and a deep sense of powerlessness over her inability to make healthy changes and stick with them. She is no longer physically active, in part because she lives in a climate that makes outdoor activities difficult to enjoy. To compound matters, Jennifer is worried about her long term health and her husband, who she raves about and adores, is at his wits end that she isn't taking care of herself.

All these factors fuel Jennifer's negative self-image which makes change even more daunting. Her confidence in her own ability to turn the ship around is at rock bottom.

It's not hard to see the figure-eight type looping between Jennifer's emotional state and her physical state. The worse she feels the worse she eats which fuels her negative emotions and poor health. And around it goes. Compounding the issue is that these habits have now morphed into a kind of identity. Consciously or subconsciously, she identifies as the woman who doesn't take care of herself and can't change. She's used to relating to herself that way and she's used to others relating to her that way as well. There is comfort in her discomfort. Her habits are causing her pain but they are familiar and that creates a kind of security and certainty. Beyond them lies the unknown. She may be afraid that she will be trading the devil she knows for the devil she doesn't. So what is the way out?

Interestingly, when I asked Jennifer to name one or two things that boost her energy, she revealed to me that when she taps into her spiritual side, she is happier and able to gain some level of control over her poor eating habits. When she was living in a spiritually nurturing environment, she was more active and was able to lose 15 pounds over several months and felt better about herself and her life overall.

As Jennifer's story illustrates, humankind has a deep connection with food that goes far beyond the need for sustenance and survival.

At times we have an almost interpersonal relationship with food. We love it. We hate it. We want it. We need it. We label it bad. We label it good. We label ourselves somewhere along the moral spectrum depending on what and how much we eat. Food taunts us. It comforts us. It numbs us. It's a tumultuous relationship.

In fact, our very humanity is reflected in that relationship.

Food is love. We show care, support, love and a sense of common humanity by preparing and sharing food with one another.

Food is memory. The more senses we engage at any given time, the stronger the memory of that moment will be in our minds. Food is a multisensory human experience - smell, sight, and taste - so it helps us remember some of life's most meaningful and magical moments.

Food is identity. Food is a way to connect to our heritage and to our own cultural identity. It is where we come from and who we are. It can also be where we want to go.

Food is faith. The first and only challenge that God presented to Adam was related to food, suggesting that there is something about food that goes to the core of the human psyche. Spiritual ceremonies in almost all faiths have aspects related to food, lending support to the notion that food can transcend the physical, crossing over to the spiritual. Cultures throughout the world have specific foods that are eaten in times of mourning and in times of joy.

Food is art. Crafting and presenting beautiful, healthful, delicious food is an art and form of creative expression with limitless possibilities.

Food is creation. Feeding the world is a creative partnership with God: raw materials, essential elements, plus human ingenuity and resourcefulness. Despite the fact that God only provides humans with the wheat stalks, the Talmud teaches that the benediction for bread thanks God for "taking bread from the Earth." The implication is clear. When we take wheat stalks and grind them, knead them into a dough, and bake them, we become partners with God in the remarkable creation called bread.

Food is bonding. We come together for a wide range of occasions over food. It is a way to share life together: the good, the difficult, the meaningful, the playful, and the professional.

Food is communication. Sharing a meal with others can bridge gaps and improve understanding of one another.

Food is joy. A multi-sensory form of pleasure.

In other words, food is a gift that comes in many forms.

EAT TO LIVE OR LIVE TO EAT?

But we have altered that gift considerably in the last century. Some of that change is positive in that we have the ability to feed the entire world. But there is a downside as well. Our eating habits have changed drastically since the mid 20th century and our minds, bodies and souls are struggling to function well despite those changes.

Today, 73% of the US food supply is ultra-processed. Americans spend 10 percent of their disposable income on fast food and the average American consumes 130 pounds of sugar in a year. That is equivalent to about 3 pounds per person per week. Where food once nourished our bodies and our souls, where we once ate locally and wholesomely, today our food choices are weakening our systems and creating food addictions.

Even if we do commit to eating more healthfully, we suffer from a very conflicted world of nutrition information. Do we eat paleo, vegan, Mediterranean, gluten-free, Keto? Do we eat small meals frequently or follow intermittent fasting? Do we eat local and seasonal or whatever is on sale at the store? The struggle is real. It's very difficult for us to know what is really good for our bodies and what isn't or to figure out how to strike a healthy balance between all the roles food plays.

In addition to the practical confusion around food, we have created tremendous spiritual dissonance around how to relate to our bodies. Do we glorify fit or fat? Do we encourage healthy habits or do we push junk food, supplements, and drugs that will save us from our unhealthy habits? Is food about health, pleasure, comfort or convenience? Do we eat to live or do we live to eat?

The latter dichotomy dates back to the beginning of the human story when Adam and Eve were challenged in the Garden of Eden. God tells them that they can enjoy all the fruits of the garden but forbids them from eating the fruits of the Tree of Knowledge. They are told that eating those fruits will lead to death. Despite this warning and a clear choice to refrain from eating the forbidden food, they ate from it because Eve *"saw that the fruit of the tree was good for eating and pleasing to the eye."* (Genesis 3:6) The fruit looked so enticing that they chose instant gratification over the long term benefit of not dying.

There is one other significant spiritual challenge given today's food choices. Because highly palatable food (think high fat, sugar, salt and starch) is cheap, ubiquitous, and addictive, it is natural and easy to turn to food to fill emotional or spiritual voids in our lives. When our hearts or souls are hurting due to lack of attention and care, food is right there to catch us. And catch us it does - for a brief moment of pleasure and comfort. But then it can often lead to a self-destructive loop from which it is hard to escape. And that's true for disordered overeating as well as under-eating.

In Jennifer's story that opened the chapter, when her disordered eating became unmanageable, she turned to a spiritually-based program to begin healing. Jennifer joined Overeaters Anonymous (OA), a 12-step recovery program founded on the principles of recovery for Alcoholics Anonymous. Like all 12-step protocols, OA is grounded in the recognition of a higher power and focuses on spiritual concepts such as acceptance, forgiveness and letting go of control. It seems then as if overcoming physical addictions requires a spiritual focus. How do we understand that?

NOURISH YOUR SOUL

The Bible relates that Isaac was elderly and the time came for him to transmit the spiritual blessings that he received from Abraham to his own son. What does he do to prepare himself for this elevated spiritual moment? He instructs his son, *"Prepare the tasty food that I love and bring it to me for me to eat so my soul can bless you before I pass away."* [Genesis 27:4] Isaac makes a clear association between eating and his ability to tap into his soul to bless his son.

All the major faiths include food as part of the spiritual worship such as the Seder feast on Passover, bread/wafers and wine for Communion, and Eid al-Fitr meals during Ramadan. All three major monotheistic faiths also understand that spiritual growth can be achieved through holding back from eating as seen from the fasts of Lent, Ramadan, and Yom Kippur.

> *Food is not just sustenance—it is a connector between the physical body and the spiritual realm.*

> Rabbi Hagai London, author of numerous books about the teachings of Rabbi Abraham Isaac Kook, explains that the Hebrew word for bread, "lechem," comes from the word "halchama" which means welding and connecting. Bread, representing the staple of diets throughout history, serves as a connector between the physical body and the spiritual realm.[74] As King Solomon writes, *"A righteous person eats to satisfy his soul."*[75]

How does this connection work? What relationship could there be between physical food and spirituality?

"If our heart and mind are focused on experiencing food as a love note from God, eating becomes not only a way to nourish and love ourselves, but each meal becomes a time for enhanced spiritual awareness and gratitude to God...Eating consciously is a way of opening one's heart to God. It is a way to feel the Divine presence." - Dr. Gabriel Cousens

The Talmud in Tractate Berachot [55a] goes as far as comparing the table upon which we eat food to the altar that was used for ritual worship in the Temple in Jerusalem.[76]

DIVINE SUSTENANCE

God created a world of indescribable natural beauty. Of all the creatures on Earth, God gave human beings, and only human beings, the aesthetic sense capable of appreciating that beauty. So much so that we can draw upon it to connect with the Infinite and our souls.

The same is true for food. God could have made all food with similar characteristics. However, God created foods of all colors, shapes, sizes, flavors, and textures. He then created human beings to be drawn to the aesthetic aspect of food beyond simply the functional aspect of food, at least when given the choice. What other living being plans the way a meal is arranged and designed because it experiences heightened pleasure by how food appears or is presented? For whose benefit did the Creator make food with such sensory variety? That additional aspect of our relationship with food means we have greater potential for gratitude, appreciation, and awe, all states of being conducive to spiritual connection.

> *When we nourish ourselves with mindfulness and gratitude, each meal becomes an opportunity to experience the Divine presence and to elevate our physical act of eating to a spiritual experience.*

Taking a step back to the most basic level, eating can be a spiritual experience because of the opportunity it provides to express gratitude to God. As the Bible says outright, *"And you shall eat and be satisfied and bless the Lord your God."* (Deuteronomy 8:10). People of all faiths and backgrounds recognize the Divine gift of nourishment and pause to pray before enjoying a meal. Recognizing that we are not the ultimate source of our food and acknowledging that it is a gift from a spiritual source is, itself, an experience that uplifts the soul.

There is another aspect to food and soul that is unique to human beings. We are not simply consumers of food. We are co-creators in the Godly act of feeding the world.

Rabbi Elchanan Wasserman, a Polish Talmudic scholar who was murdered by the Nazis during the Holocaust, described a scene in which an alien comes to Earth and witnesses a farmer's work as he seeks to produce bread. The alien watches in astonishment as a beautiful green field is torn up by a plow and replaced by seeds that get buried into the ground. But then after a period of time, stalks begin to grow. He is shocked as he watches the farmer cut down the impressive looking stalks, beat them, dump them into a pile, and grind them up. But then when the alien sees that the farmer kneads what is left from the stalk and creates loaves, he thinks the work has been done. But he is then horrified again as he sees the farmer take those loaves and put them into a fiery furnace. The alien is able to breathe a sigh of relief when the farmer takes the wonderful smelling bread out of the oven and places it on the table for consumption.[77]

We are truly co-creators with God when it comes to food cultivation and preparation. The process is astonishing. Some would say miraculous.

Equally miraculous is how our bodies are designed to enjoy and break down food, warn us when food is no longer healthful, digest and withdraw the nutrients needed for our survival, and expel the waste, all through an intricate and integrated biological system. Our omnivorous teeth allow us to eat a variety of foods; saliva and enzymes help us smoothly swallow our food, taste buds on the tongue send nerve impulse to the brain to taste the food; the epiglottis covering the windpipe pushes the food down the esophagus instead of into the lungs; the stomach, liver and pancreas extract the positive elements of our food to nourish us while disposing of the dangerous elements which can cause us harm; and 15 feet of intestines which enable the final disposing of the waste from our food intake.

With all this to reflect on, meal time becomes an ideal opportunity for appreciating the wisdom of creation. And that leads us back to recognizing our spiritual roots.

As Job poignantly and succinctly remarked, "From this body I see God." [19:26]

But the food-soul connection goes deeper than that.

MYSTICAL MEANING OF FOOD

Kabbalah points out that the Hebrew word for food, "Ma'achal," is made up of the exact same four letters as the Hebrew word for angel, "Mal'ach." (The Hebrew letters are "mem," "lamed," "aleph," and "chof") In mystical thought, an angel is the tool and mechanism through which God interacts with the world. Our food, whether the source is crops that grow from the ground or animal life, is connected to the Divine source that created it to begin with. This means that, similar to an angel, the food, itself, brings its Creator into the world and infuses that Divine spirit into our bodies when we eat the food.

18th century Hasidic master, Dov Ber ben Avraham of Mezeritch, also known as the Maggid of Mezeritch, takes this concept one step further. The Bible teaches that *"Man does not live on bread alone, but by the utterance of God's mouth does man live."* (Deuteronomy 8:3). Rabbi Dov Ber explained this verse based on the Kabbalistic teaching that the letters of Divine speech that served as the the instrument for the creation of every item in creation, are nestled inside each of those creations. When a person is hungry and seeks to eat a specific food item - this is actually a reflection of the soul craving a connection to the Divine utterance that is the "soul" of the food item. (This, of course, refers to foods in their natural state or close to it, as opposed to processed foods with close to zero connection to anything God created.) Thus while we think we are desiring and enjoying a merely physical food, in actuality we are seeking and gaining from the spiritual connection to "God's utterance," latent inside the food which God created.[78]

Circling back around to the practical level, given the variety of choices and structured diet plans available, how do you find the best way of eating for you? How do you harness the power of food to maximize your overall well being - physical, spiritual and emotional? The answer is a soulful one. You have to get quiet and listen - not to the television or to the latest social media influencer or to advertisers or even to well meaning friends. You have to tune in to your own inner wisdom.

DOV'S FOOD JOURNEY

I am a strict vegetarian and try my best to maintain a vegan diet. This was most certainly not the way I always ate. My father struggled with controlling his weight throughout my upbringing and that led to him going on numerous diets and made the topic of weight very present in the home as far back as I can remember. But it was from a perspective of weight gain and weight loss, not from an overall wellness perspective. As a result, since I didn't struggle with my weight as a child and teenager, I never gave a moment's thought to what I was eating, aside from adhering to rules of Kosher.

Then in my early 20's I noticed that I was starting to gain weight in an unhealthy manner. I began to pay more attention to what I was eating, most specifically by cutting back on unhealthy (and unnecessary) snack foods. I was still slightly overweight but that, along with regular exercise, stopped me from becoming severely overweight.

Then in 2014, while serving as a member of Knesset, I learned about the health and environmental benefits of cutting back on meat consumption. Those revelations, combined with concerns that I had about the treatment of animals during the production of meat, dairy, and eggs, led me to my current diet. In addition, I try to keep to intermittent fasting, not eating for 14 hours between dinner and breakfast. I hold back on cakes, cookies, and sugar-laden drinks throughout the week but allow myself to enjoy these in small amounts on the Sabbath.

It is not simple to eat healthily while on this diet since it involves eating a lot of carbs and soy based products which are not healthy in large amounts. I also take B12 supplements and have regular blood tests to make sure I am getting all the nutrients that I need. I can for sure say that aside from keeping my weight down, I feel healthier overall with this approach to eating. I never have the weighed down feeling one gets after a solid meat meal and I feel lighter, more energetic, and happier.

In terms of the impact of my diet on my spirituality, for starters, the very fact that I feel good about myself physically and feel happier, frees me to grow and connect spiritually. But on a deeper level, combining the discipline and thought which goes into what and when I will and won't eat means that I am connected to myself and my needs throughout my day. Finally, going back to the Sabbath, I used to eat so much [we officially eat three bread based meals during the 25 hour Sabbath] that it took away from spending the day in spiritual pursuits. Now that I eat less and never feel overly stuffed, it frees me to spend large parts of the Sabbath day in spiritual study and reading as opposed to sleeping and tending to stomach related challenges.

ATARA'S FOOD JOURNEY

My journey with food has not been simple. Like my client at the beginning of the chapter, my eating habits and my sense of self got confounded in my teenage years. I struggled with low self-esteem, anxiety and a deep-seated sense that my body was my worth. The thinner my body, the greater my worth. Focusing on my food (or lack thereof) and exercise was an escape from the tensions at home and in my own mind, heart and soul. It became an almost spiritual quest for me - an intelligent, sensitive (and soulful) kid trying to escape and make sense of her own life.

In terms of environment, I grew up in the fitness industry of the 80s where super thin was all the rage. Anorexia was almost cool. I fit right in. I was a certified fitness instructor by 17 years old, a high school cheerleader and track runner. I rarely sat down. To add to that, at home there was subtle messaging that there was an optimal weight I was supposed to be at for my parents to be comfortable. If I was too thin, that was an issue. If I gained weight, that was noticed as well. Other people's weight was also a topic of conversation.

On the positive side of the ledger, my parents are both very health conscious. They are avid exercisers, healthy eaters who eat moderate amounts of food, and enjoy time outdoors. I grew up with a palate accustomed to lots of fresh fruit and vegetables, balanced meals, and very little processed or junk food. We ate out very occasionally - meals were always homemade and fresh.

I never officially got help for my eating disorder and body dysmorphia. I just evolved into a better place with time. Like other addictive ways of thinking I don't know if it ever really leaves you completely. But I have worked hard to find a way of eating that makes sense for my body and mind. I've tried vegetarian, macrobiotic, no-carb, low-carb, gluten-free, intermittent fasting, even the-pizza-and-chocolate diet when I was pregnant. What determined my food choices were my priorities at the time. Sometimes it was quieting my anxiety. Other times it was a way of eating that supported my athleticism or maintained my weight. Now I am working on finding a way of eating that supports graceful aging, reduces inflammation and tames my autoimmune disorders. I always eat healthfully but exactly what macronutrients I focused on changed with time and circumstance.

There was one more step in my food journey that started over 25 years ago. In 1997, I became religiously observant and was introduced to the concept of kashrut - the idea that what and how we eat can have a direct connection to our spiritual growth. Today, I eat (primarily) a natural, whole foods omnivorous diet. I haven't owned a scale in decades. I say a blessing before and after I eat to experience and express gratitude to God for all the blessings food provides. And I focus on the power of food to heal and support all that I want to accomplish in this lifetime.

YOUR FOOD JOURNEY

Given all of the various factors that impact our food choices, How do you figure out the best way for you to eat?

Like movement and spiritual pursuits, there is no one size fits all for food. You have to tune into your own body and learn to hear and accurately interpret what it's telling you. That is a new skill for many people. Like all new skills, it requires practice and intent to successfully change how and what we eat. It's also important to be aware of the snare of fast foods and highly palatable packaged foods that can scramble the signals and create cravings, even addictions. So slowing down, getting quiet, and being mindful about what and how you eat becomes the foundation of making good food choices for your body and your life.

Rather than making any particular food or food habit the enemy, the following exercises will open a door to a new relationship with food. We are each here for a purpose and that purpose is supported by a healthy body, a peaceful mind, and a vibrant spiritual core. Meal and snack times, like so many things in life, are an opportunity to bring all parts of yourself to the table, literally and figuratively, and connect with the spiritual side of eating. Bon appetit!

MEDITATION #5
FOOD AS A PATHWAY TO SOUL

As we mentioned above, everything in the natural world contains a spark of the divine and can be a conduit for spiritual connection and growth. That includes food and how we nourish ourselves.

The following three meditations - two for before you eat and one for after you eat - are designed to elevate the physical experience of eating to a spiritual level and to connect you to the Divine. We invite you to bring all your senses - touch, smell, sight, taste and hearing - as well as your sixth sense, your intuition or spiritual center - to the table with you when you next eat.

For these meditations to be most impactful, choose meals when you can create the time and ability to focus and reflect.

Pre-eating:

a) Honor the origins of your food

Pick one food on your plate. Close your eyes and imagine the very first step that had to be taken for this food to be in front of you right now. Did it start as a seed that had to be planted? An animal that had to be raised? A fruit that had to be picked? How many ingredients are in this food? Where did the foods originate? How far did they have to travel? How did they all come together?

Close your eyes and picture each of the steps that led to it sitting in front of you. The Divine wisdom that went into creating a universe in which the seed becomes food. The work the farmer did to prepare the land, plant the seeds, nurture the soil, harvest the crops, and prepare them for shipping. The truckers that drive the goods to the market or to the factories. The workers and equipment needed to process and package the food. The shipping and the stocking in the grocery store.

You may choose to be aware of gratitude for everyone and everything involved in the cultivation and preparation of this item of food. If so, holding the gratitude in your heart, take a bite of the food. As you begin the physical act of chewing, tasting, and swallowing the food, reflect on and give thanks to the Divine and to all those who helped bring this food to your table today. Whether you choose to thank a different part of the process with every bite or let feelings of gratitude wash over you throughout the meal, observe any feelings or sensations that come up.

b) Mindful eating

Begin by connecting to your breath and your body. Feel the chair underneath you and your feet touching the floor. Take a slow breath in and a long, slow exhale. Notice any sensations in your body, the temperature of the room, any sounds you hear, any emotions you are feeling. Bring yourself to this place and this moment with full presence.

Imagine that you are seeing the food in front of you for the first time. Notice the color, shape, texture, and size. Feel the texture and temperature. Is it smooth or rough, sticky or solid, hot, cold, or room temperature?

Again, notice if you have any thoughts, sensations or emotions at this time. Continue to breathe and be fully present in this moment.

Take the piece of food and bring it toward your nose and inhale deeply. How does your mind and body react to the smell of the food? While paying attention to your hand moving towards your mouth, place the object into your mouth without chewing or swallowing it. Just allow it to be in your mouth, moving it to different parts of your mouth and tongue. Notice the flavor and texture. Notice the physical sensations within your body, especially your mouth and your gut. Continue to breathe as you explore the sensation of having this item in your mouth.

Swallow.

Then take the next piece of food and take a bite. Notice the flavor, notice the change of texture. Then very slowly begin to chew this piece of food. When you are ready, swallow this item and notice the path that it follows from your mouth and throat into your stomach. Notice the sensation and taste that may linger in your mouth.

Connect again to your body and your breath and notice your experience in this moment.

After meal or snack

Set your utensils down and close your eyes. Take a slow deep breath in and a long exhale out. Check in with your body. How do you feel right now? Do you feel sated, full, overfull, still hungry, thirsty? Do you feel heavy or sluggish? Relaxed? Energized?

Now check in with your heart. What emotions are coming up for you right now? What feelings would you like to express?

Now check in with your soul. What wisdom around food wants to be expressed right now?

Many spiritual practices encourage a moment of gratitude and reflection prior to eating. Interestingly, however, the Bible teaches us to express thanks *after* eating., "When you have eaten and are satisfied, you shall bless the Lord your God." (Deuteronomy 8:10) When we are sated, we become comfortable and more inert. That heavy, satisfied feeling can lead us to taking the gift of food and its Divine source for granted. But if we pause and appreciate the blessings that food provides - satisfying hunger, providing us with the energy that we need, and giving pleasure - it can be a moment of significant gratitude.

Take one more moment to consider the intricate design of your digestive system, all of which happens involuntarily. If any small aspect of this process doesn't run smoothly, it becomes quickly apparent in the form of discomfort, indigestion or disease. You may choose to be aware of gratitude for a healthy digestive system. This post-eating meditation reminds us to be thankful and acknowledge God's blessings when life is full and satisfying and not just when we are needy.

The interconnectedness of our body and soul can provide a wonderful tool for living a meaningful, soul based life. It means that making positive changes in how we care for our bodies - like eating nourishing and strengthening foods - builds our sense of self-respect as well as improving our absolute physical state. That in turn creates positive emotions and greater bandwidth for spiritual pursuits. Conversely, if you are struggling more existentially, feeding and caring for the soul can give you the perspective you need to let go of stress, tension and control which relaxes the body and allows you to make better food choices, sleep better, have more energy, and lead a happier and more fulfilling life.

CHAPTER TEN

YOUR CHILDREN AND SOUL

[**Dov**] *Daniel was a problematic student. He was that student that all young teachers dread having in their classroom. Irreverent. Disrespectful. Uninterested. Unfazed by disciplinary action. His presence was hurtful to the classroom and the school at large. After numerous suspensions, expulsion was on the table. And then, it all changed. The school visited a senior citizen's home to bring the elderly some pre-holiday happiness. The idea was for students to sing, hand out gifts, and interact with the residents. This is a scary experience for most teenagers. Many of the elderly suffered from physical ailments which could make students uncomfortable. Other residents had advanced dementia and blurted out random, at times inappropriate, declarations. The teens all stood to the side with sheepish and frightened looks on their faces. Nothing was happening. Until Daniel stepped forward. His irreverence empowered him to lead. He began to sing. He began to dance. He began to make the residents laugh. That broke down the barrier for the other students and they all joined in. And this also broke down the barrier for Daniel to get his life on track Volunteering and giving to others became his passion. It was his source of joy. It led him to find meaning in his life. And that led to his taking life and learning more seriously. His parents provided him with food, shelter, and many other material needs and gifts. But like a car with just three wheels or a house without a roof, a critical piece of Daniel hadn't been activated, thereby hampering his development. We as teachers also failed to give him what he so desperately needed. But that day at the senior citizen's home, he found it for himself. That was when he found the key to his soul. And he has never been the same.*

OUR CHILDREN NEED MORE

As parents, we love our children. But they are struggling. Now more than ever before.

Consider some of the recent statistics on the state of our children's mental and physical health:

In a 2020 SAMHSA study, the age group with the highest prevalence of serious mental illness was adults ages 18-25. A whopping 49.5% of all adolescents ages 13-18 were diagnosed with a mental disorder of some type in a 2001-2004 study.[79]

Suicide is the second-leading cause of death among people age 15 to 24 in the U.S. Nearly 20% of high school students report serious thoughts of suicide and 9% have made an attempt to take their lives, according to the National Alliance on Mental Illness. 'The things that make them vulnerable are where they stand socially and where they stand developmentally,' says UCLA Health's Dr. Carl Fleisher.[80]

In the United States, drug overdose death rates in 15-24 year-olds increased four-fold from 3.2/100 000 to 12.6/100 000 between 1999 and 2017.[81]

The statistics on our children's physical health aren't much better:

Between 2000 and 2016, the proportion of overweight or obese children (age 5-19) doubled from one in ten children to one in five.[82] In addition to other diseases and disorders, obesity has been correlated with depression and anxiety in children and youth, with females at a higher risk than males.[83] Overweight children are also more likely to have social challenges such as being bullied or bullying others, poor self-esteem, and cognitive and academic challenges.[84]

In recent years, children are being diagnosed with a range of health conditions previously only seen in adults such as type II diabetes, high cholesterol and high blood pressure, sleep disorders, and eating disorders such as anorexia and bulimia and fatigue.

In these areas, our children are struggling for the same reasons adults are struggling - poor quality diet, lack of exercise, too much screen time, little to no time in nature, lack of positive social support, and lack of stress management skills. This scenario creates a triple threat to children's overall wellbeing - cognitive, emotional, and physical.

Please see Appendix D on page 111 for more on the importance of raising children with healthy dietary and physical activity habits

While each child's strengths and struggles are unique, it seems clear that many of our children are missing something, even suffering. And while they know they don't feel good, healthy and happy, they don't know what to reach for to feel better. So they go "lookin' for love in all the wrong places." What are they searching for that they are filling with food, internet, drugs, alcohol, violence, and risky behaviors?

Like Daniel, they might just be searching for their souls.

A GIFT FOR OUR CHILDREN

Giving and acts of service were Daniel's entry point to a spiritual connection with himself and others. He harnessed his strengths, which until the senior citizen's home masked themselves as challenges, channeling his energy to building rather than break down. What if Daniel hadn't had this opportunity? What are we offering our children to help them connect with their spiritual selves?

According to Dr. Lisa Miller, author of *The Spiritual Child: The New Science on Parenting for Health and Lifelong Thriving*, "Spirituality is an inner sense of relationship to a higher power that is loving and guiding. The word we give to this higher power might be God, nature, spirit, the universe, the creator, or other words that represent a divine presence. But the important point is that spirituality encompasses our relationship and dialogue with this higher presence."[85]

There may be no greater gift we can give our children today than the ability to connect lovingly with their own soul and a desire for a relationship with the Divine.

The greatest gift we can give our children is the ability to connect lovingly with their own soul and a desire for a relationship with the Divine.

Children who are raised with a positive spiritual foundation are more likely to possess character traits such as resilience, empathy, optimism, and industriousness. They understand their own value and respect and appreciate the value of others. They are grounded in an awareness that there is purpose to their lives and method to the world's madness. They are better equipped to view challenges through a wider lens and they are often driven by a sense of greater good and responsibility. In other words, spiritually attuned children have more tools in their toolbox as they grow and mature.

Rabbi Yakov Danishevsky, a licensed clinical social worker, shares a simple yet profound idea for raising soul-centered children. When children come home from school, it's common for a parent to ask a child about his or her scholastic achievements for the day. "How was your test?" "What did you learn today?" "How much homework do you have?" These questions, while certainly understandable, all focus on a certain type of success, namely academic. If those are the first, or indeed only, questions we ask our kids, we are saying that we value what they can produce. Contrast this with the following questions: "How did you help someone today?" "What challenge did you overcome today?" "What are you grateful for that happened today?" These questions send the message that who the child is and how the child acts is a primary value in the home.[86]

Before going further into this, it is important to remember that children are hard wired to want to be loved, seen, appreciated, and cared for unconditionally by their parents above all else. Those needs are true even when children become adults. As you consider the concepts in this chapter, remember that it's never too late to work on a relationship. It's never too late to work on ourselves to be better people and better parents. The past is in the rear view mirror but the future is wide open.

[Atara] *I asked my three children what advice they would give to parents about how to raise spiritually healthy children. Their answers appear throughout this chapter.*

Yaeli, 18, a student replied: *"I think tradition has a lot to do with building a spiritual foundation. If kids understand and are taught over and over again the value of your parents and your grandparents and your great grandparents and all your family history, you understand that you are a part of something greater. You don't just exist in a vacuum in your life right now. I think that would be a really depressing thought that everything I do right now just exists right now and tomorrow it doesn't go towards anything. That any of my actions just exist in this moment and don't have so much of an effect. But if you emphasize where you come from and how far back you go, you realize you are a link in a very, very long chain and you are enabling that chain to keep going. You have almost a responsibility to keep that going. That means your actions matter as a part of something bigger."*

Is it even possible to raise spiritually healthy children in our times when the competition for our children's souls is so fierce? Our kids are bombarded by various sources of media, much of which have little to offer in the way of positive, soul-affirming messaging. And we, as parents, may not be equipped to model a spiritually-based life. There is also a general downtrend in religious affiliation in the 21st century which means fewer and fewer families lean into formalized spiritual practices as well. So is all lost?

The answer is a clear and resounding no!

NATURAL SPIRITUALITY

For starters, children are naturally inclined towards spirituality.

The Cognition and Theology Project of the Center for Anthropology and Mind at Oxford University studied children in a wide range of cultures in both traditionally religious and atheist societies. The analytical and empirical research, which involved 57 researchers in 20 different countries, suggests that children's cognitive systems may be especially receptive to certain god concepts and concluded that "humans are predisposed to believe in gods and an afterlife" from birth.

The Oxford Study concludes: *"Recent research suggests that even 12 month olds understand that only intentional beings create order from disorder (Newman, et al., forthcoming). Not surprisingly, then, children have a strong bias to see the world as purposefully designed."*[87]

Boston University Professor Deborah Kelemen asserts that children may be 'intuitive theists' and show evidence of being "teleologically promiscuous", meaning that young children lean towards understanding the physical world in terms of meaning and purpose rather than simple function.[88]

The sages of the Talmud understood this reality and taught that before a child is born, the soul is able to "see from one end of the world to the other." [Niddah 30b] Rabbi Yaakov Greenwald, a 20th century Israeli teacher and philosopher explains this to mean that, "Before the soul comes into this physical world it perceives the entire universe as a single unit, a single revelation," under the orchestration of a Divine Being.[89]

We also see a child's natural spirituality through their (enviable) wide-eyed curiosity, awe of the universe, openness, truthfulness, and capacity to love - all soulful qualities. If you've ever walked through the woods with a child, you'll notice that it takes a very long time to go a very short distance. Every bug, every leaf, every puddle, every oddly shaped rock, every tree root is fair game for touching, tasting, sitting on, plucking out, squishing or rolling around in. As adults, we may appreciate the quiet, the beauty, and the grandeur, but we also might think about if we have on the right gear, if our bug spray works against ticks, and what we need at the grocery store for dinner.

The openness and curiosity of a child, that presence in the now, are inherently spiritual qualities. They reflect a wonderment and a desire for connection through understanding. They are the same traits that underscore those awkward moments when a child verbalizes a thought or a question about someone they are observing that turns everyone in earshot a different shade of red.

All this "good news" translates into a reality that as parents, we don't have to create something from nothing. We just have to nurture what is inherently present.

How do we do that?

The Talmud teaches that there are three partners in the creation of every human being - the mother, the father, and God. The soul is gifted by God, who then charges the parents with loving, nurturing, and accompanying that soul on its spiritual journey.[90]

In other words, it starts with *us*.

SPIRITUAL PARENTING

Parents lead first and foremost by example.

In the words of Dr. Daniel J. Siegel, clinical professor of psychiatry at the UCLA School of Medicine and executive director of the Mindsight Institute, *"As children develop, their brains 'mirror' their parent's brain. In other words, the parent's own growth and development, or lack of those, impact the child's brain."*[91]

Our children are constantly observing us. So when it comes to the spiritual development of our children, we must walk the walk. If we as parents live our lives with a focus on the spiritual, our children will see the consistency in our messaging and are likely to follow.

So the first step of spiritual parenting is to understand your own relationship with your soul.

Much of this book is intended to help you build that critical foundation. Armed with an understanding and appreciation of the spiritual discovery process, you can be a positive and empathetic role model for your child's own spiritual development.

The second step in spiritual parenting is opening up and nurturing a dialogue around spiritual growth. Proactively speaking to our children about our connection to spirituality has its roots all the way back to the Bible itself. The Book of Exodus records that God told Moses that the Israelites should tell "the ears of [the] children" about their salvation from Egypt so "they will know that I am God." [Exodus 10:2]

Rabbi Yaakov Weinberg explains that God was teaching that there is benefit in sharing spiritual inspiration with children who don't yet have an ability to comprehend the actual words or concepts. Just the sound waves entering their ears have an impact. Like drops of water over time can reshape a stone, speaking to children from the youngest ages about spirituality helps them to "know God" and grow up with recognition of the spiritual dimension.

As the Oxford study posits, talking to our children about a higher power reinforces what they know intuitively. If we don't talk about it, a child's spiritual inclination can atrophy, making them less sensitive to spirituality as adults.

Baila [Weisberger] Farkash, 22, teacher, on raising a spiritually healthy child: *"I think to raise a spiritually healthy child it's important to reaffirm that there is something bigger than yourself. I think in this world we are so focused on diets and clothing and this and that and it can really really feel like you are literally just a body in this world. I think to be able to say to your child, 'Wow, I'm so lucky that God gifted me with such a beautiful soul like you' or to say we are 'trying to do xxxx because we are trying to be better people' - making the goal of childhood to turn them into a better person - helps build a child spiritually. If a parent is hyper focused on the physical aspects of their child- like the way they look or the way they dress - it can start to chip away at the child's sense of self, leaving them feeling like 'I'm just a body and that's all that matters.' Having a spiritual focus - that there is a greater purpose to things, that there is a God above you, that 'I'm so lucky God gave you to me' - starts to build a language for kids and a vocabulary for the concept and helps them to see themselves as both a body and soul."*

Sharing your spiritual efforts and experiences is a third powerful tool for spiritual parenting. For example, if you connect to your spiritual essence most profoundly in nature, bring your children into that experience with you. Let them know what those experiences mean to you. If family or tradition or music or meditation or helping others connects you, share with your children that you are choosing to incorporate these into your life in order to enhance your spirituality.

If spiritual parenting prepares the soil for planting, the seeds of a spiritual child are respect for the child's uniqueness, love, patience, and joy.

ACCORDING TO THE CHILD'S WAY

King Solomon taught *"Educate children according to their way."* [Proverbs 22:6] Six words. Six words that can change worlds.

As convenient as it would be, God doesn't come down to the world and tap each of us on the shoulder as children and say, "Listen kid, your mission in life is XXXXX. I gave you this and that ability and these parents so that you can fulfill your mission. Now go get it."

Rather, God imbues each soul with a unique set of talents, interests, abilities, and personality. The primary responsibility rests on the child to discover these and use them for their individual life journey. But the charge for parents is to recognize and appreciate the uniqueness in their children and lean into those unique strengths in the education process. This is particularly true in the realm of spiritual education.

The Bible tells the story of the births of twin brothers, Esau and Jacob, to Isaac and Rebbecca. It describes that *"The boys grew up, and **behold** Esau was a skillful hunter, a man of the field, and Jacob was a simple child who sat in tents."* [Genesis 25:27] The Bible is very clear about how the story ends: Esau left the path of Abraham's legacy and created his own life path, while Jacob was crowned as "the destiny child" to continue the monotheistic traditions of Abraham, fathering the twelve tribes of Israel.

Rabbi Samson Raphael Hirsch, a 19th century educator and Bible commentator, teaches that Esau's non-spiritual life path which led him away from Abraham's legacy was not due to his nature but a failure in nurture. Hirsch notes that the word "behold" when the boys grew up demonstrates that Isaac and Rebecca were not aware of the differences between the character traits of the boys and raised the two exactly the same. And that mistake had devastating spiritual consequences for Esau. *"Had Isaac and Rebecca studied Esau's nature and asked themselves…how even an Esau…could be won for endeavors in the service of God… that mighty man would not become [merely] a mighty hunter, but truly a mighty man before God."* Rabbi Hirsch asks, had Isaac and Rebecca studied the true nature of each of the boys, and guided Esau to embrace his interests and talents and directed them to spiritual pursuits, *"Who knows what a different turn all of history would have taken?"*[92]

One of the most powerful ways to build a sense of spirituality in our children is to study their natures, and to recognize and support their gifts and talents as a reflection of their soul and purpose.

LOVE

[**Dov**] *Twenty-five years educating religiously observant teens has introduced me into the lives of thousands of students. I have seen it all. Some thrived spiritually and physically, while others had to struggle and work hard to overcome immense personal and spiritual challenges. Some successfully overcame their challenges while others never managed to get themselves on track. I have also been blessed to raise four very different children and, as an involved dad, had a front row seat to their challenges and those of their friends.*

I fully recognize that no solution is foolproof, and I have seen how even the best of parents suffered as their children chose unhealthy and unspiritual lifestyles and life paths. There also comes a time when we as parents sometimes have to very painfully let go and allow our children to become their own, independent individuals. That being said, I have seen a correlation between how parents live their lives and interact with their children, and how the children live their lives.

The parents of my students who were loving, caring, and involved in their children's lives and interests tended to have children who were far more disciplined and willing to hear what their parents had to say, especially when it came to spirituality. And when those loving and involved parents modeled healthy and soul focused behaviors, their children tended to follow in their path.

Love is the foundation of all that is good in the world. It is also what creates the rich soil required for all of our positive parenting efforts to take root and grow. When it comes to health and wellbeing, there is simply no substitute for showing your kids how much you love them. A 2019 Harvard study found that students who said they grew up with warmth and caring from their parents were healthier socially, emotionally, and psychologically than those who did not experience that parental warmth. Those who felt their parents' love were less likely to engage in harmful or risky behaviors like drugs and smoking, and experienced greater positive emotions and healthier relationships.[93]

The Grant Study, which began in 1938 and followed 268 Harvard graduates for 75 years, determined that children who had warm relationships with their fathers as children showed lower rates of anxiety as adults and greater "life satisfaction" when they were 75 years old.

Dr. Christina Bethell, a professor and researcher involved with a 2019 Johns Hopkins study on this topic sums up its bottom-line conclusion: *"When a child is met with loving, attuned, and responsive relationships on a moment-by-moment basis, they are literally learning that life is safe; that they matter; that others can be trusted. With this, they can feel safe and stay open to explore, be curious, learn and interact with other people in a positive way."*[94]

Please see Appendix E on page 113 for more on the correlation between loving parents and their children's physical health

Yaakov Weisberger, 21, musician: *"Be supportive of your child. The best thing you can do for their spirituality is to provide a safe, loving and caring upbringing. If you're a good parent and are loving and supportive, the rest will follow. Never force your beliefs on them just because they don't gravitate to it naturally. Spirituality and beliefs are personal and should never be infringed upon by the parents. It's totally ok to raise them a certain way but if they start to stray as they get older because a different spiritual outlook or way of life suits them better, don't stand in the way or try to influence them the other way. Oftentimes they may even come back to the way of life that they were raised to follow anyways. Be supportive and loving. Those are the main things. Nothing else really matters."*

This sense of safety extends to the spiritual as children gain the self-worth to not only explore the outside world but to look deeper into themselves as well. This opens a pathway necessary for them to discover and identify with their spiritual cores.

PATIENCE

Another spiritual trait to develop as we strive to raise soul-focused children who seek to lead meaningful lives is patience.

Rabbi Shlomo Wolbe, a 20th century ethical and spiritual guide in Israel teaches that there are two ways to view raising children: building and planting. When a builder lays a brick you see the results right away. That immediate gratification is thrilling. But that brick can never sporadically create a new brick on its own. In contrast, planting involves plowing, digging, watering, and waiting. You start with a small seed, and with time and patience a tree emerges, and that tree has the capacity to produce its own fruit.[95]

We naturally focus on how our child is acting in the present. And parents have a tendency to worry about and micromanage the here and now. But that perspective is like the builder who lays the brick and rightfully expects to see the building going up right before his eyes. We have to remember that while, of course, we hope our child acts properly now, what is truly important and essential is how the child grows into the future. We want to raise children who will grow into that tree that can then produce its own "fruit" for themselves and the world. Like the seed placed into the ground, it may take a long time for them to get there. And the process may involve a lot of sweat and tears. At times it may feel like that seed will remain in the ground forever and amount to nothing. But we know that with patience and the right nurturing - love, care, focus, spiritual teaching and modeling, and yes, prayer - the seed will eventually surface and the child will become that fruit bearing tree.

Rabbi Lawrence Keleman offers another analogy to help us lean into patience with our children and give us hope in hard times. In his book "To Kindle a Soul," he reminds us that the seed must rot before it sprouts. Those moments when our children are struggling, when they seem disinterested in anything meaningful or productive, or even worse, are getting themselves into trouble, may be part of a child's development process. Some children can only reach great heights by first experiencing serious lows. Our job as parents is to internalize that the only thing that ensures the plant will die is stopping to water and nurture it. And the only chance the seed has to grow into that fruit bearing tree is to lovingly tend to it.[96]

SEEING YOUR CHILD AS A SOUL

[Dov] *The passing of my 7-month-old granddaughter, was and is devastating. I don't believe losing a child or grandchild is a loss that you ever "get over." That being said, we are blessed with the capacity to pick ourselves up and move forward after these tragedies. Though the pain never goes away, the acuteness and intensity of it softens with time. Loss is never just about pain. There are always important* lessons to learn from tragedy. For me, Ruti's passing was a life altering event in terms of how I now see my children and especially my grandchildren. She had charm, exuded joy, and demonstrated love. When I looked at her lifeless body which no longer conveyed those qualities, the reality that those traits were reflections of her soul became glaringly clear to me. Until that moment I knew intellectually that the essence of my offspring was their souls, but I saw them as their physical realities and not as souls. Now when I look at them and interact with them, I almost always either naturally or quickly remind myself that I am interacting with a soul that happens to be in a physical body. Seeing them through this lens gives me the capacity to be more patient with them, to try to dig deeper and understand what is going on for them beneath the surface, and to try to focus on how I can best contribute to their soul journey.

JOY

A joyful home is a healthy home. That doesn't mean a Pollyanna type of joy where issues get swept under the rug or real feelings aren't encouraged or expressed. It doesn't mean there aren't struggles or challenges. Creating joy means that parents look for and express the good. It means spending quality and enjoyable time together. It means expressing gratitude regularly and sincerely. It's creating an atmosphere where a child wants to be. Without joy, it is challenging to transmit values to our children that will stick as it is normal for a child to move away from negative or painful associations. A warm and joyful home is the perfect incubator in which goodness and spiritual values can grow.

Yael Weisberger: "One of my teachers, Rabbi Berkowitz, says that the commandment to be joyful comes from the commandment to love God (Deuteronomy 6:5). You find the commandment of being joyful **in** the commandment of loving God. When you love God and you realize that there is a God, that brings you to happiness. And you realize you can't really have happiness without a God or without some sort of spirituality and you can't have spirituality without happiness and it goes hand in hand. In order for that, you have to instill that into the house and you do that by finding the good in life and pointing it out and appreciating it. p.s. If the whole purpose of life is to love God, then the whole purpose of life is to be joyful because they're hand in hand."

EXERCISE #8: FAMILY DINNER EXPERIENCE

The Dinner Concept

Where can love, planting, and learning more about your child come together in one place? Around the dinner table! As hard as it can be to get schedules in sync (or even to get kids on board), family meals can nurture and nourish more than just your bodies. It's an opportunity to connect and communicate with your children, learn about your children's interests, and to create a loving atmosphere in the home where children feel seen and valued.

If this is a new practice for your family, frequency is less important than consistency. Pick the same night each week when you will all sit down together so you and your children can plan your schedules around the family dinner experience. That consistency and predictability will help make this new practice become a family tradition! Below are suggestions for making the most out of the family dinner experience as well as conversation prompts to get your kids talking. Again, like every new behavior, it may feel awkward at first. But repetition breeds comfortable familiarity with time!

Suggestions for Success

If you know your family's favorite foods, the weekly dinner is a great time to make them! If you don't know which foods your kids would be most excited about, ask them for their three favorite meal choices. You can round robin the choices by week or by child.

As challenging as it might be for adults and children alike, having a 'no phones at the table' policy for this one meal a week will be a game changer in terms of connecting. You can explain that the goal is for the family to spend quality time together and, therefore, phones will be put aside during dinner.

Share positive experiences that you had during that day and week and also ask your children about their day and their week. Talk sports. Talk entertainment. Talk current events. Talk about what your children want to talk about.

Listen to what your children say with open curiosity and without judgment. If they open up and then feel criticized for what they share, they won't feel safe sharing again.

The family dinner experience doesn't have to be long or drawn out. Quality over quantity is definitely the goal.

Conversation Prompts

What was your highlight from this past week?

What's a choice you made this week that you are proud of? What are you excited about right now?

Genie in a bottle: What's one wish you would ask for?

If you could hit the rewind button and do something over again from this past week, what would you do differently?

What did you do to help someone else this week?

What are you grateful for?

What was the best part of your day/week?

Post dinner reflections:

What did you learn about your children this week during the family dinner experience? What did they learn about you? What learning can you carry over into the coming week based on the conversation at the dinner table?

Let's remind ourselves that no matter what they say, our children will *always* look to us as role models and guides. That being said, we can never expect our children to do for themselves what we are not willing or able to do for ourselves. *Carpe diem!*

HOW TO SOUL

RETURN AGAIN

When you were a newborn, you were completely dependent for all your physical needs. You needed others to feed you, to clothe you, to transport you , and to clean you. You could not fully see, could not fully hear, had no control over your bowels, and had no teeth to chew on food.

If as an infant you didn't have physical capabilities - no skills to act on, no success to pursue, no hobbies to enjoy, and no choices to make - then who were you? What was your identity?

When you look at a newborn baby (something we tend to do a lot of as new grandparents), it exudes spiritual purity. It projects the light and inner peace reflective of a soul that has just arrived in the world from on High. The perfect skin and perfect tiny features are a physical representation of this purity. The baby has not yet struggled, physically or emotionally, with mistakes, missteps, and the negative influences which surround us on Earth. The inability to do anything on its own, a reality which does not exist in any other living being at birth, seems to highlight this dimension of the uniquely human experience and existence - its spiritual identity. Its soul.

Fast forward to the end of life. If we are fortunate, we live well into our seventh, eighth, even ninth decade of life. But as we age, our physical selves often revert back to the newborn baby stage - struggles with eyesight, hearing, mobility, and needing partial or full time assistance.

What do these bookend lifespan experiences of dependence and limited physical capabilities tell us about the long journey of life in between? Do we go through all the ups and downs of life just to revert back to not having any physical independence, regressing to being like a newborn baby again?

"Maybe the journey isn't about becoming anything. Maybe it's about unbecoming everything that isn't really you, so that you can be who you were meant to be in the first place."

Brazilian novelist Paulo Coehlo

Soul work isn't about becoming someone different. It's about shedding the layers that never really belonged to us to return to our most authentic selves.

Oftentimes what sends us searching for our soul are the more painful realities of life, not the pleasurable ones. Challenges are there to create little cracks in the armor we've built that protect us from the tender spots inside. In those tender spots is our very humanity, the aspects of ourselves that make us who we actually are. They point us in the direction of the work we are supposed to do to become the people we are supposed to be.

It's so easy to patch up the armor and go on with our lives as we have always done. It is possible to turn away from the pain and distract or distance ourselves from the opportunity that lies in the challenges we face. We push away connecting with our authentic selves in lieu of asserting our acquired selves, the selves we've developed to feel safe, accepted and loved. But then we miss the opportunity to grow and deepen our relationship with our own soul.

Now we can reframe the "regression" to physical dependence in our senior years from the negative to the positive. . Yes, it might mean requiring varying degrees of assistance which no person enjoys. But in spiritual reality, the shedding of the physical identity which so dominated our lives allows for returning to that very spiritual space. That place of purity, calm, and light that reflects the return to our source which truly feels like home. There is a reason why every single description of a near death experience includes a description of light, warmth, and inner peace.

So, all of life seems to set us on a journey toward returning again. In the words of the song "Return Again" written by Jewish composer and singer Shlomo Carlebach, our life mission statement is to "Return to who you are, return to what you are."

And therein lies the great challenge. If we allow the natural flow of life on Earth to take over, we will find ourselves striving for wealth and success, seeking the admiration and adulation of those around us, and identifying ourselves based on our physical bodies and appearance. The inner peace and spirituality which marked our entry into the world quickly dissipates. But whether we like it or not, the cycle of life takes us back to who we were when we were born - closer to spiritual reality rather than physical reality.

Whether you are in a life transition, looking for greater meaning and purpose, struggling with a challenge, or just looking to learn and grow, we commend you for picking up *How to Soul* - for honoring the voice inside that wants to live more authentically. It takes courage to explore uncharted territory within ourselves and we tip our hat to you for getting curious about what is possible.

It is our hope and prayer that "How to Soul" has given you the perspective and tools to take that challenge and transform it into an opportunity. All of life can be a soul journey. All of life can tap into that pure spirituality with which you entered the world and where you will head toward in your later years. That spirituality can serve as your guiding light as you navigate the ups and downs of life so you are constantly returning to who you are and what you are. And it is that returning again that can help fill your life with inner peace and purpose.

HOW TO SOUL

APPENDIX A

ADDITIONAL GUIDANCE REGARDING FINDING THE COURAGE TO MAKE SIGNIFICANT DECISIONS

Rabbi Dr. Abraham Twerski writes that there are six factors which make it difficult for us to change course in our daily living: Denial, Rationalization, Habituation, Projection, Trivializing, and Ego.

The prophet Isaiah explains that **denial** means that we, as humans, intentionally and selectively close our eyes and ears to certain realities in front of us. When speaking to the ancient Israelites, Isaiah says that the nation does so "lest it see with its eyes and hear with its ears and understand with its heart, so that it will change course and be healed." (Isaiah 6:9-10)

Rabbi Twerski explains that "No psychology text can improve on Isaiah's description of denial. Because people are intent on doing whatever they wish, they resort to denial, one of the best-known defense mechanisms so that they are unaffected by the reality of what they see and hear. We are creatures of habit, and we are comfortable when we can do things without the need to exert much effort. Change is uncomfortable, and in order to avoid this discomfort, our minds block out the realizations that might call for change."[97]

Moving onto the second element, Rabbi Twerski explains, "When reality threatens to overcome denial, the mind employs other defense mechanisms to reinforce the denial—such as **rationalization.** One of the themes in the Book of Proverbs is the tendency to rationalize…Denial is not always possible, so the mind is very clever in rationalizing; in other words, justifying one's actions by giving logical-sounding reasons for them."

The third factor is **habituation.** The Talmud teaches that once we do something which we know is wrong a few times, in Rabbi Twerski's words, "it loses its opprobrium…[One's] conscience is lulled into thinking, 'it's really not so terrible.'"

The defense mechanism of **projection** blames others for the problem. "It's my parent's fault, what can I do about it?" "Work and time constraints are the reasons I can't exercise." "The social system is broken." "I was pressured to do it."

A fifth factor is **trivializing,** reducing the importance, significance or complexity of a more serious issue. [Describe what trivializing means here]. Examples of trivializing are: "It wasn't even a big deal." "No one will care anyhow." "Lots of people live long lives who don't live healthy lifestyles." "I can stop whenever I want."

Rabbi Twerski elaborates in depth on the sixth factor which he labels as **ego.** "One of the axioms of human behavior is that a person will always choose to do that which is most comfortable for him. We find that an addict will not agree to change until he hits "rock-bottom," i.e., that the pain incident to the addiction is greater than the pleasure it provides. This is equally true of the non-addict. Therefore, oftentimes individuals only agree to change when they have reached rock-bottom.

But what can constitute rock-bottom for the non-addict? A person who contemplates his life goals and sees that his behavior is jeopardizing his reaching those goals may reach rock-bottom. But this requires giving serious thought to defining one's goals and purpose in life."[98]

APPENDIX B

MODERN DAY NATURE-RELATE THERAPIES

Ecotherapy, a growing scientific field, has demonstrated a strong correlation between spending time in nature and a reduction in stress, anxiety and even depression. A 2015 study explored differences in the brain activity of healthy people following a 90-minute walk in nature versus the same in an urban setting. The results demonstrated that walking in nature lowers activity in the prefrontal cortex, the part of the brain that responds to depression with repetitive negative thoughts and emotions.

The science also indicates that the calming sounds of nature and the silence of the outdoors lowers blood pressure and cortisol levels, one of the primary stress hormones. In a 2017 study, researchers measured the brain activity of people as they listened to the sounds of nature versus when they listened to artificial sounds. MRI scans indicated that when hearing artificial sounds, the brain reacted with an inward-directed focus, the way it functions when one experiences anxiety, PTSD, and depression. When the person listens to the sounds of nature, the brain responds with an outward-directed focus, more typical functioning during restful, peaceful moments like daydreaming.[99]

A host of nature-based therapies have developed out of this research. Animal therapy, using service animals to help people with mental health conditions, has proven to be extremely effective. A 2019 study found that Canine-Assisted Psychotherapy (CAP) is particularly helpful in assisting adolescents in need of mental health treatment. CAP serves as a positive intervention for internalizing disorders with internal manifestations of distress such as anxiety, depression, anger, and PTSD, as well as for externalizing disorders that present with external displays of distress such as aggression, impulsivity, rule breaking, and inattention.[100]

Similar results were found with Equine Therapy (ET), using horses for mental health treatment. ET has been found to help people of all ages, particularly adolescents struggling with assertiveness, confidence, developing and maintaining relationships, emotional awareness, empathy, impulse control, problem-solving skills, social skills, trust in others, and trust in self.[101]

Wilderness Adventure Therapy (WAT), which uses a wide range of challenges and experiences in nature, is another treatment that has shown to improve mental health. A 2016 study determined that WAT has positive impact on a wide range of mental health challenges including depression, anxiety, social problems, withdrawal, coping, problem solving, self-esteem, and even suicidality.[102]

APPENDIX C

ADDITIONAL INFORMATION AND DATA ABOUT THE CONNECTION BETWEEN PHYSICAL ACTIVITY AND MENTAL/PHYSICAL HEALTH

The National Weight Control Registry, the largest database ever assembled on individuals successful at long-term maintenance of weight loss, shows the extent to which our physical activity level has dropped. According to the NWCR, from 1988-2010, the proportion of U.S. adults *NOT* exercising regularly went from *19.1% to 51.7%* for women and from *11.4 to 43.5%* for men.

There is mounting evidence that a lack of movement is a contributing factor in nearly every modern disease and mental disorder we know about. According to the National Institutes of Health, lack of physical activity is a primary cause initiating 35 separate pathological and clinical conditions, including loss of functional capacities with chronological aging; metabolic syndrome, obesity, insulin resistance, prediabetes/type 2 diabetes, non-alcoholic liver disease, cardiovascular diseases, cognitive functions and diseases, bone and connective tissue disorders, cancer, reproductive diseases, and diseases of the digestive tract, lungs, and kidneys.[103]

Aside from its correlation to physical illnesses, the decrease in physical activity runs parallel to the increase in anxiety and depression.

Depression and anxiety disorders, one of the leading causes of disability worldwide, cost the global economy $1 trillion each year in lost productivity. 1 in 5 U.S. adults experience mental illness. A full 19% of Americans suffer from an anxiety disorder. 18% of U.S. adults with mental illness also have a substance use disorder.[104]

Even before COVID-19, the prevalence of mental illness among adults was increasing. In 2017-2018, 19% of adults experienced a mental illness, an increase of 1.5 million people over the previous year's dataset. Suicidal ideation among adults is also increasing. 460,000 more adults experienced serious thoughts of suicide in 2017-2018 than they did in 2016-2017.[105]

According to a report in 2011 by the National Center for Health Statistics (NCHS), the rate of antidepressant use in America among teens and adults (people ages 12 and older) increased by almost 400% between 1988–1994 and 2005–2008.[106]

While correlation does not imply causation, it is hard to imagine that there is no connection between our decreasing levels of physical activity and the increase in anxiety and depression. As we lean more and more into technology, that pattern may continue unless we actively seek to counter it. As the world faces a mental health crisis, effective, sustainable, and accessible solutions are essential.

In general terms, our level of physical activity is shown to be positively associated with general well-being, lower levels of anxiety and depression, and positive mood. This relationship is independent of the effects of socioeconomic status and physical health, and applied to younger and older members of both sexes. The association is particularly strong for women and people aged 40 years and over.

In a 2019 study published by JAMA Psychiatry, running for 15 minutes a day or walking for an hour reduces the risk of major depression. Study author Karmel Choi, a clinical and research fellow at the Harvard T.H. Chan School of Public Health, cites a "26% decrease in odds for becoming depressed for each major increase in objectively measured physical activity."

In a 2008 study, researchers found that even low levels of physical activity improved mood for people with serious mental illness, such as bipolar disorder, major depression and schizophrenia.[107]

The robustness of this conclusion stems from the nature of the data sources: four population samples in two countries over the span of 10 years in which physical activity levels were assessed by four techniques and psychological status was assessed by six distinct scales.[108]

The role which increased physical activity plays in protecting against stress-related mental disorders is well documented. One study examines whether young adults who fulfill the American College of Sports Medicine's (ACSM) vigorous intensity exercise recommendations differ from peers below these standards with regard to their levels of perceived stress, depressive symptoms, perceived pain, and sleep. Those who followed the more rigorous exercise plan demonstrated less stress, pain, complaints about sleep, and depressive symptoms. In fact, the vigorous exercisers had more favorable overall sleep patterns including increased total sleep time, more stage 4 and REM sleep, more slow wave sleep, and a lower percentage of light sleep. The vigorous exercisers also reported fewer mental health problems when exposed to high stress.[109]

Other studies show that regular aerobic exercise is associated with lower sympathetic nervous system and hypothalamic-pituitary-adrenal (HPA) axis reactivity. The HPA axis controls reactions to stress and regulates many body processes, including digestion, immune response, mood and emotions, sexuality and energy storage and expenditure. Dysregulations in the HPA axis have long been implicated in the manifestations of depressive and anxiety symptoms.

Exercise is also a powerful stress reducer, lowering levels of the body's stress hormones, such as adrenaline and cortisol. High levels of adrenaline and cortisol increase stress reactions but also increase blood sugar and can fuel both cravings and weight gain, particularly in the higher-risk abdominal region. It is not hard to see how this dynamic creates a negative emotional loop: stress - increased adrenaline and cortisol - food cravings and feelings of anxiety - poor food choices - weight gain and poor impulse control - additional source of stress - increased adrenaline and cortisol - and the loop continues.

It's physical activity that can break that negative pattern.

When we increase our heart rate through physical activity, we change our brain chemistry, increasing the availability of important anti-anxiety neurochemicals, including serotonin, gamma aminobutyric acid (GABA), brain-derived neurotrophic factor (BDNF), and endocannabinoids. Exercise activates frontal regions of the brain responsible for executive function, which helps control the amygdala, our reacting system to real or imagined threats to our survival. In other words, in contrast to the negative feedback loop described above, physical activity creates a positive emotional feedback loop. When we are active, we have lower amounts of stress hormones and increased 'feel good' hormones. Our executive functioning capacity is higher which means we make better choices for ourselves. We end up feeling more relaxed, more confident in our choices and avoid the unwanted secondary impacts of stress including weight gain.[110]

As the case for physical activity builds as a first line of defense for mental health, what keeps us from embracing a more active lifestyle? Why aren't we jumping on the exercise bandwagon wholeheartedly?

There are a number of reasons why we turn away from the evidence.

The first reason is the structure and mindset of the current modern medical system. Western medicine is outstanding at critical care. But when it comes to resolving chronic illness and promoting lasting wellness, it has been far less successful. Patient-clinician interactions tend to follow a pattern of symptom, compartmentalized diagnosis, prescription, side effect, additional prescription, and around it goes. Nowhere in modern medicine has this pattern been clearer than in the area of mental health.

In the absence of laboratory tests to diagnose mental health conditions, clinicians are forced to take a 'throwing darts' approach to pharmaceutical treatment of mental disorders and disease. Choose a dart, throw it, and see where it lands. Doesn't work? We have many other darts to throw. Side effects? "I can give you something for those too." While psychiatric medications certainly have value as one option for treatment of mental disorders, taking the 'silver bullet' approach is like giving insulin to a type II diabetic and ignoring the long-term necessity for lifestyle change. Mental illness has physical, emotional, mental and spiritual components so the universal focus on medication as the go-to treatment misses the mark on so many levels.

Therapy can also be an effective treatment for mental health and responsible clinicians will advise patients not to rely exclusively on pharmaceutical fixes to change their reality. But therapy can take a long time to work, if it works, and it's a trial-and-error process as well to find the right clinician for any given patient.

With all that said, we have a drug in our arsenal that is powerful, proven to be effective, inexpensive, accessible, provides immediate relief, and is free of negative side effects. Yet it is rarely prescribed as a first line of treatment.

That drug is physical activity.

Come with us for a moment into the world of possibility. What would happen if before a psychiatrist prescribes a pharmaceutical drug, patients are given a physical activity prescription and are required to walk for 30 minutes a day in the fresh air? What if insurance companies provide and require the use of an inexpensive activity tracker before they approve a prescription drug for depression, anxiety, or ADHD? What if psychiatrists and therapists were to practice as a team with health coaches, exercise specialists, mindfulness practitioners and nutritionists to treat the whole person? What would long-term outcomes look like in this scenario?

Yes, medical school and residency training would have to adapt and change. Pharmaceutical companies would have to level up their mindset and approach - dramatically. But if the goal of the medical establishment and medical companies is truly the long-term wellbeing of patients, we must insist that the mental health system evolve towards a more integrative approach. There is no doubt that in the face of a powerful drug lobby, clinicians that are trained to medicate, and patients that know nothing other than to expect prescriptions as the first line of treatment, we have our work cut out for us. But the first step to change is recognizing the problem and exploring a holistic approach - at least for ourselves.

There is a second factor why we resist embracing physical activity as a first line of treatment for mental health. It is also why prescription drugs can seem much more appealing: the prospect of *change*.

Change is far more complicated than taking a pill. It requires more thought and more effort for the patient and the clinician. Moreover, when the pill fails, you can blame the physician and/or the drug companies. When we fail to achieve positive change through our own efforts, we can only blame ourselves. And that doesn't feel good.

There *are* clinicians that make lifestyle suggestions. But those recommendations often land with a dull thud at the feet of the patient. Why? Because patients are inherently unmotivated? No. Everybody is motivated by something in life. Rather it's because generalized, top-down directives don't work when it comes to lifestyle and behavior change. It isn't a lock and key relationship. Lifestyle change is messier than that. And modern medicine doesn't have the time or the bandwidth for messy. Messy also doesn't come with a medical code.

In the Academy Award winning animated film, WALL-E, Axion is a Pixar-designed luxury spaceship that carries "the last refuge of a consumer culture, a self-contained world built by the Buy n' Large Corporation, loaded with excess and wandering adrift with the remnants of human race." The humans on board the Axiom have "settled into a life of pampered luxury...floating around on their high deck chairs" and consuming volumes of junk food. The two dystopian aspects to WALL-E are interrelated: the destruction of the earth by over-consumption and waste and the self-destruction of the human race through a life of excess, comfort, convenience and lack of movement.[111]

Every dystopian film has a thread of truth running through it that reflects aspects of our current reality. And while the end-of-the-earth-by consumption vision of WALL-E can and should be debated, we cannot ignore its message regarding the damage that we are doing to ourselves (the Earth) and humanity as a result of consumerism, excess materialism and inertia.

The third reason we turn away from the evidence connecting movement to mood is a dislike of formal exercise. Many people perceive exercise as uncomfortable, inconvenient and time consuming. They also assume that if you are not huffing, puffing, and sweating it out at the gym, that there is no benefit to less formal forms of movement. While there is tremendous value for the mind and body in a challenging workout, exercise is not a zero-sum game. Any movement is better than no movement. It's not all or nothing. It's every little bit counts. In other words, movement lies along a continuum with sedentary at one end and intense exercise on the other end. In between is a huge range of types of movement that are beneficial for the mind and body including walking, gardening, dancing, climbing stairs, stretching, cleaning, playing with children, swimming, mowing the lawn (not seated of course), hiking, carrying groceries and more. Any movement that raises your heart rate and engages your muscles and joints counts.

For those who appreciate concrete numbers as guidance, according to the Mayo Clinic, the recommendation for exercise is at least 150 minutes of moderate aerobic activity (a bit more than 20 minutes per day) or 75 minutes of vigorous aerobic activity a week (a bit more than 10 minutes per day), or a combination of moderate and vigorous activity. The recommendation is that you spread out this exercise over the course of a week so that you get some physical activity daily. Greater amounts of exercise will provide even more benefit but short bouts of physical activity are beneficial as well.[112]

In terms of integrating more movement into your life, there is another consideration. We tend to be creatures of immediate gratification, especially at times when life is stressful or challenging. If we don't enjoy exercise to begin with and we try and motivate ourselves to exercise so that we can achieve some down-the-road benefit (like weight loss), it becomes even more difficult to get ourselves moving. The beauty of exercise in relation to mental and emotional health is that the benefits of exercise are immediate. You may feel better minutes into moving or you may feel better afterwards simply by knowing you did something good for yourself. In either case, you feel the benefits in the moment and that is a powerful motivator to get moving.

APPENDIX D

THE IMPORTANCE OF RAISING CHILDREN WITH HEALTHY DIETARY AND PHYSICAL ACTIVITY HABITS

A 2014 NIH study found evidence of a significant, cross-sectional relationship between unhealthy dietary patterns and poorer mental health in children and adolescents. They observed a consistent trend in the relationship between good-quality diet and better mental health and some evidence for the reverse.[113]

The U.S. Food and Drug Administration has approved more than 10,000 additives which the American Academy of Pediatrics (AAP) determined can interfere with hormones, proper growth and development of children. The AAP's "Food Additives and Child Health" policy provides a list of these additives, including synthetic artificial food coloring, and their negative impacts which can have negative impact on child behavior and attention, and nitrates which studies have linked to tumors in the digestive and nervous systems, interference with the blood's ability to deliver oxygen in the body, and can cause thyroid problems.[114]

The scientific evidence also points to the importance of a child's diet from the earliest of ages. The quality, quantity, timing, and nutrient components of meals impact a child's physical and mental health. Nutrition can either have a positive or negative impact on cognitive development which then influences attention, perception, learning and memory. Children who grow up regularly eating foods with high fat and high carbohydrate content often struggle with obesity which leads to increased risk of cardiometabolic disease in adolescence and adulthood. Obesity in the childhood years can also lead to the premature development of diseases such as liver disease, type 2 diabetes, and osteoporosis. Childhood obesity also negatively impacts confidence and inability to be physically active which impacts physical and mental health.[115]

The Center for Disease Control recommends that children ages 6 through 17 years old do 60 minutes or more of "moderate to vigorous intensity physical activity" on a daily basis that includes aerobic and strength training. However, according to the CDC, less than one in four children gets this recommended physical activity.[116]

Physical activity in early childhood has a direct impact on the cognitive and social development of children along with their physical and mental health. Even among children under one year old, their physical activity has an influence on their motor skill development and weight management later in life. Among toddlers, from one to three years old, movement builds bone and skeletal health. The reverse is also true. High levels of sedentary behavior among children in their early years has a negative impact on their health. High amounts of screen time among children under the age of four relates to decreased cognitive development, irregular sleep patterns, increased weight challenges which can lead to disease, and decreased psychosocial health. Even more significantly, the evidence is clear that the habits that children develop at the earliest of ages tend to continue into later childhood and adolescence.[117]

APPENDIX E

CORRELATION BETWEEN LOVING PARENTS AND THEIR CHILDREN'S PHYSICAL HEALTH

The long-term positive impact of parents showing love, caring and warmth to their children is not limited to the mental and emotional wellbeing of their kids. A 1950 Harvard Mastery of Stress Study followed the lives of Harvard graduates for 35 years. 91% of those who reported not having a warm relationship with their mothers during their college years - defined as loving, friendly, warm, open, understanding, sympathetic and just - ended up suffering from midlife diseases such as coronary artery disease, ulcera, hypertension and alcoholism while only 45% of those who had positive relationships with their mothers had these diseases.[118]

Overall, 29% of the students who gave their parents high ratings for caring for them were diagnosed with diseases midlife while the percentage of those who rated their parents low in terms of caring for them and developed diseases midlife was a staggering 95%![119]

… HOW TO SOUL

ENDNOTES

1. Rhodes, Brianna, and Brianna Rhodes. 2019. "Deion Sanders Opens up About Hitting 'Rock Bottom,' Suicide Attempt." TheGrio. March 29, 2019. https://thegrio.com/2019/03/28/deion sanders-rock-bottom/.

2. Sanders, Deion. 2021. "Letter to My Younger Self by Deion Sanders." The Players' Tribune, October 14, 2021. https://www.theplayerstribune.com/articles/deion-sanders-letter-to-my younger-self.

3. *The Artscroll English Tanach: Stone Edition: The Jewish Bible.* United States: Mesorah Publications, Limited, 2011.

4. Ahmed Z, Zeeshan S, Mendhe D, Dong X. Human gene and disease associations for clinical-genomics and precision medicine research. Clin Transl Med. 2020 Jan;10(1):297-318. doi: 10.1002/ctm2.28. PMID: 32508008; PMCID: PMC7240856.

5. Luzzato, Moshe Chaim. *Mesillas Yesharim*. Israel: Feldheim, 2004.

6. S, Pangambam. 2020. "Oprah Winfrey'S 2015 Harry'S Last Lecture at Stanford University (Full Transcript)." The Singju Post. June 15, 2020. https://singjupost.com/oprah-winfreys-2015- harrys-last-lecture-at-stanford-university-full-transcript/?singlepage=1#.

7. *Pirkei Avos*. United States: Mesorah Publications, 1984.

8   Sifra, *Kedoshim*, Ch. 4. Sefaria: A Living Library of Jewish Texts Online, February 11, 2025. https://www.sefaria.org/Sifra%2C_Kedoshim%2C_Chapter_4.1?lang=bi.

9   Weinberg, Yaakov. *Personal Communication.*

10 Wolbe, Shlomo. *Personal Communication.*

11 Kook, Abraham Isaac. *The Spiritual Revolution of Rav Kook: The Writings of a Jewish Mystic.* Israel: Gefen Publishing House, 2018.

12 Midrash Tanchuma Pekudei 38:3

13 Wineberg, Yosef. *Lessons in Tanya: The Tanya of R. Shneur Zalman of Liadi* .... United States: Kehot, 1987.

14 Kook, Abraham Isaac. *Shmonah Kevatzim* 7:81

15 Kaplan, Aryeh. *Jewish Meditation: A Practical Guide.* United States: Schocken Books, 1985.

16 "Parashat Lech Lecha: Ideology Vs. Theology | the Eden Center Podcast Episode on Amazon Music," n.d. https://music.amazon.com/podcasts/e1241d3b-eff6-48ca-bc9b-c362c94a1e25/episodes/13e9bc1f-5194-4375-9c8e-6687313b76a4/the-eden-center-podcast-parashat-lech-lecha-ideology-vs-theology.

17 Soloveitchik, Joseph Dov. *Abraham's journey: reflections on the life of the founding patriarch.* United States: Toras HoRav Foundation, 2008.

18 *Talmud Bavli.* Sanhedrin 37a.

19 Wolbe, Shlomo. *Alei Shur, Vol. I, p. 168.*

20 Turner, Kelly A., PhD. 2014. *Radical Remission: Surviving Cancer Against All Odds.* HarperOne.

21 Yehuda Aryeh Leib Alter, *Sfat Emet.*

22 Luzzato, Moshe Chaim. *Mesillas Yesharim.* Israel: Feldheim, 2004.

23 Sinek, Simon. 2018. The Infinite Game. https://library.stiami.ac.id/?p=show_detail&id=11679.

24 Ballard, Chris. 2022. "Inside LeBron's Grand Plan to Play in the NBA With Bronny and Bryce - Sports Illustrated." SI, August 30, 2022. https://www.si.com/nba/2022/08/30/lebron-bronny bryce-james-daily-cover.

25 Twerski, Abraham J. 1999. *I Am I*. Shahar Press.

26 Raz, Simcha. *Kochav Hashachar.* Jerusalem: Gefen. 1988

27 "Technophobe George Clooney's Phone Fury." Washington Post, January 12, 2023. https://www.washingtonpost.com/entertainment/technophobe-george-clooneys-phone-fury/2015/05/19/f169bdfc-fe00-11e4-8c77-bf274685e1df_story.html.

28 Bretherton, Inge. 1992. "The Origins of Attachment Theory: John Bowlby and Mary Ainsworth." Developmental Psychology 28 (5): 759–75. https://doi.org/10.1037/0012-1649.28.5.759.

29 Jane R. Dickie, Amy K. Eshleman, Dawn M. Merasco, Amy Shepard, Michael Vander Wilt and Melissa Johnson. "Parent-Child Relationships and Children's Images of God." "Journal for the Scientific Study of Religion , Mar., 1997, Vol. 36, No. 1. pp 25-43.

30 Teshuvot haRashba, part V 51. n.d. https://www.sefaria.org/Teshuvot_haRashba_part_V.51?lang=en.

31 Will, George F. 1990. Men at Work: The Craft of Baseball. http://ci.nii.ac.jp/ncid/BA11511923

32 Kook, Abraham Isaac Hakohen. 2024. *Hadarav: His Inner Chambers*. Maggid.

33 Luzzato, Moshe Chaim. *Mesillas Yesharim*. Israel: Feldheim, 2004.

34 Luzzato, Moshe Chaim. *Mesillas Yesharim*. Israel: Feldheim, 2004.

35 *Talmud Bavli*, Niddah 16b.

36 Covey, S. R., and D Blankenhagen. 1991. *The 7 Habits of Highly Effective People.* Performance + Instruction 30 (10): 38. https://doi.org/10.1002/pfi.4170301009.

37 Shapira, Kalonymus Kalman. *To Heal the Soul: The Spiritual Journal of a Chasidic Rebbe*. United States: Jason Aronson, Incorporated, 1995.

38 Yaakov ben Asher. *Arba'ah Turim*. 14th century.

39 Neff, Kristin. 2003. "Self-Compassion: An Alternative Conceptualization of a Healthy Attitude Toward Oneself." Self and Identity 2 (2): 85–101. https://doi.org/10.1080/15298860309032.

40 *Pirkei Avos*. United States: Mesorah Publications, 1984.

41 Maimonides, *Mishneh Torah*, Yesodei HaTorah 7:4

42 Hladik, Matt. "Klay Thompson's Postgame Quote About the Ocean Goes Viral." The Spun, July 10, 2024. https://thespun.com/nba/golden-state-warriors/klay-thompsons-postgame-quote-about-the-ocean-goes-viral.

43 Maimonides, *Mishneh Torah*, Avodat Kochavim 1:3.

44 Maimonides, *Mishneh Torah*, Yesodei HaTorah 2:2

45 Stein, A. David. *A Garden of Choice Fruit: 200 Classic Jewish Quotes on Human Beings and the Environment*. United States: Shomrei Adamah, 1991.

46 Davis, Mary. *Every Day Spirit: A Daybook of Wisdom, Joy and Peace*. United States: Sourcebooks, 2024.

47 Monroy, Maria, and Dacher Keltner. 2022. "Awe as a Pathway to Mental and Physical Health." Perspectives on Psychological Science 18 (2): 309–20. https://journals.sagepub.com/doi/full/10.1177/17456916221094856.

48 Marvelly, Paula. 2023. "Ralph Waldo Emerson: Nature | the Culturium." The Culturium. September 3, 2023. https://www.theculturium.com/ralph-waldo-emerson-nature/.

49 *A Treasury of Jewish Poetry*. United States: Crown Publishers, 1957.

50 Bissell, Ronald D. 1998. *Unity: Life's Essence*. Inner Voice Productions.

51 Goldhill, Olivia. 2022. "Astronauts Report an 'Overview Effect' From the Awe of Space Travel —and You Can Replicate It Here on Earth." Quartz, July 21, 2022. https://qz.com/496201/astronauts-report-an-overview-effect-from-the-awe-of-space-travel-and-you-can-replicate-it-here-on-earth.

52 Ulrich, Roger. (1986). Human Responses to Vegetation and Landscapes. Landscape and Urban Planning. 13. 29-44. 10.1016/0169-2046(86)90005-8.

53 Harvard Health. "Sour Mood Getting You Down? Get Back to Nature," March 30, 2021. https://www.health.harvard.edu/mind-and-mood/sour-mood-getting-you-down-get-back-to-nature.

54 Ecclesiastes Rabbah 7:28. "Kohelet Rabbah 7:28," n.d. https://www.sefaria.org/Kohelet_Rabbah.7.28?lang=en.

55 Hirsch, Samson Raphael., Elias, Joseph. *The Nineteen Letters*. Israel: Feldheim Publishers, 1995.

56 *Talmud Bavli*, Arukhin 36b.

57 *Talmud Yerushalmi*, Kiddushin 4:12.

58 Barnett, Samantha. "The Quill of the Soul - the Power of Music," n.d. https://www.chabad.org/theJewishWoman/article_cdo/aid/1388688/jewish/The-Quill-of-the-Soul.htm.

59 Music for the Soul. 2024. "What Science Is Telling Us | Music for the Soul." Music for the Soul. August 30, 2024. https://www.musicforthesoul.org/healing-music-guide/what-science is-telling-us/

60 Harvard Health. "Music Can Boost Memory and Mood," February 14, 2015. https://www.health.harvard.edu/mind-and-mood/music-can-boost-memory-and-mood.

61 Judah Loew ben Bezalel (Maharal), *Tiferet Yisrael* 2:1.

62 Quora. "Why Does Music Touch Your Soul?," n.d. https://www.quora.com/Why-does-music-touch-your-soul. https://qr.ae/pY9LuU

63 Maimonides, Moses. 2010. *The Guide of the Perplexed*, Volume 2. University of Chicago Press. Parshat Beshalach, Chapter 8.

64 Luzzato, Moshe Chaim. *Mesillas Yesharim*. Israel: Feldheim, 2004.

65 Millis, John P., PhD. 2019. "Can a Planet Make a Sound in Space?" ThoughtCo. July 25, 2019. https://www.thoughtco.com/is-there-such-a-thing-as-a-planet-sound-3073443.

66 *Midrash Livnat HaSapir*, Kings II 3:15.

67 "Devarim Fall 2020 9 a Poem as Testimony | Sefaria," n.d. https://www.sefaria.org/sheets/283606.

68 *Talmud Bavli*, Berachot 32b.

69 Maimonides, *Mishneh Torah*, Hilchot De'ot 4:15

70 "Podcasting, Daily Practices, and the Long and Winding Path to Healing - Brené Brown." 2024. Brené Brown. January 17, 2024. https://brenebrown.com/podcast/brene-with-tim-ferriss-and-dax-shepard-on-podcasting-daily-practices-and-the-long-and-winding-path-to-healing/.

71 Dadlani, Roshni. "Why Is Exercising Important to Feel Good? — the MINDS Foundation." The MINDS Foundation, July 7, 2020. https://www.mindsfoundation.org/blog/exercising-to-feel-good.

72 Kook, Abraham Isaac. *Shmonah Kevatzim* 1:426.

73 *Personal Communication* with student of Rabbi Kagan.

74 London, Rabbi Hagai. 2023. "To Eat Bread Before God." Arutz 7, February 9, 2023. https://www.inn.co.il/news/591738?ssr=1.

75 Kook, Abraham Isaac. *Parables* 13:25.

76 *Talmud Bavli*, Berachot 55a.

77 Brody, Lazer. 2021. "The Wheat Field." Breslev.Com. June 4, 2021. Accessed February 12, 2025. https://breslev.com/332130/.

78 Chabad.org. n.d. "The Chassidic Masters on Food and Eating." https://www.chabad.org/library/article_cdo/aid/73827/jewish/The-Chassidic-Masters-on-Food.htm.

79 "Mental Illness." n.d. National Institute of Mental Health (NIMH). https://www.nimh.nih.gov/health/statistics/mental-illness.

80 "Suicide Rates Among Young People Continue to Rise, but There Are Ways to Help." 2022. UCLA Health. March 15, 2022. https://connect.uclahealth.org/2022/03/15/suicide-rate highest-among-%20teens-and-young-adults/.

81 Spencer, Merianne, Matthew Garnett, and Arialdi Miniño. "Drug Overdose Deaths in the United States, 2002-2022," November 28, 2023. https://doi.org/10.15620/cdc:135849.

82 "Poor Diets Damaging Children's Health Worldwide, Warns UNICEF," October 15, 2019. https://www.unicef.org/press-releases/poor-diets-damaging-childrens-health-worldwide-warns-unicef.

83 Quek, Ying-Hui, Wilson W. S. Tam, Melvyn W. B. Zhang, and Roger C. M. Ho. "Exploring the Association Between Childhood and Adolescent Obesity and Depression: A Meta-analysis." Obesity Reviews 18, no. 7 (April 12, 2017): 742–54. https://doi.org/10.1111/obr.12535.

84 OECD. "The Heavy Burden of Obesity," October 10, 2019. https://www.oecd.org/en/publications/the-heavy-burden-of-obesity_67450d67-en.html.

85 Miller, Lisa. 2015. The Spiritual Child: The New Science on Parenting for Health and Lifelong Thriving. https://openlibrary.org/books/OL28580580M/Spiritual_Child.

86 "The Attached Life." 2025. Apple Podcasts. January 8, 2025. https://podcasts.apple.com/us/ podcast/the-attached-life/id1664578187.

87 ScienceDaily. "Humans 'predisposed' to Believe in Gods and the Afterlife," July 11, 2011. https://www.sciencedaily.com/releases/2011/07/110714103828.htm.

88 Kelemen, Deborah and Boston University. 2004. "Are Children '"Intuitive Theists"'? Reasoning About Purpose and Design in Nature." 5. Psychological Science. Vol. 15. https:// www.bu.edu/cdl/files/2013/08/2004_Kelemen_IntuitiveTheist.pdf

89 Greenwald, Yaacov. 2020. With Truth and with Love 2: Actualizing Potential and Serving with Joy. Vol. 2. Feldheim Publishers.

90 Talmud Bavli, Kiddushin 30b.

91 Siegel, Daniel J. 2003. Parenting From the Inside Out. https://openlibrary.org/books/ OL8816401M/Parenting_from_the_Inside_Out.

92 The Hirsch Chumash: Sefer Bereshis. Israel: Feldheim, 2000.

93 "Parental Warmth and Flourishing in Mid-Life." n.d. The Human Flourishing Program. https:// hfh.fas.harvard.edu/parental-warmth

94 Zimlich, Rachael. 2020. "Positive Childhood Experiences May Have Greater Impact Than the Bad." Contemporary Pediatrics, November 13, 2020. https://www.contemporarypediatrics.com/view/positive-childhood-experiences-may-have-greater impact-bad.

95 Wolbe, Shlomo. *Planting & Building: Raising a Jewish Child.* Israel: Feldheim Publishers, 2000.

96 Kelemen, Lawrence. *To Kindle a Soul: Ancient Wisdom for Modern Parents and Teachers.* Israel: Targum/Leviathan, 2001.

97 Twerski, Abraham J. 2012. "Why Is It so Hard to Change? The Six Obstacles to Teshuvah - Jewish Action." Jewish Action. season-03 2012. https://jewishaction.com/jewish-living/why-is-it-so-hard-to-change-the-six-obstacles-to-teshuvah/.

98 Jewish Action | a Publication of the Orthodox Union, 2012b. Jewish Action. March 18, 2012. https://jewishaction.com/jewish-living/why-is-it-so-hard-to-change-the-six-obstacles-to teshuvah

99 Van Praag, Cassandra D. Gould, Sarah N. Garfinkel, Oliver Sparasci, Alex Mees, Andrew O. Philippides, Mark Ware, Cristina Ottaviani, and Hugo D. Critchley. 2017. "Mind-wandering and Alterations to Default Mode Network Connectivity When Listening to Naturalistic Versus Artificial Sounds." Scientific Reports 7 (1). https://doi.org/10.1038/srep45273.

100 Jones, Melanie G., Simon M. Rice, and Susan M. Cotton. "Incorporating Animal-assisted Therapy in Mental Health Treatments for Adolescents: A Systematic Review of Canine Assisted Psychotherapy." PLoS ONE 14, no. 1 (January 17, 2019): e0210761. https://doi.org/10.1371/journal.pone.0210761.

101 Hemingway, Ann, Sid Carter, Andrew Callaway, Emma Kavanagh, and Shelley Ellis. "An Exploration of the Mechanism of Action of an Equine-Assisted Intervention." Animals 9, no. 6 (May 31, 2019): 303. https://doi.org/10.3390/ani9060303.

102 Bowen, Daniel J., James T. Neill, and Simon J.R. Crisp. "Wilderness Adventure Therapy Effects on the Mental Health of Youth Participants." Evaluation and Program Planning 58 (May 13, 2016): 49–59. https://doi.org/10.1016/j.evalprogplan.2016.05.005.

103 National Alliance on Mental Illness. 2024. "Mental Health by the Numbers | NAMI." NAMI. September 17, 2024. https://www.nami.org/mhstats. "The State of Mental Health in America." n.d. Mental Health America. https:// www.mhanational.org/issues/state-mental-health-america.

104 National Alliance on Mental Illness. "Mental Health by the Numbers | NAMI." NAMI, February 6, 2025. https://www.nami.org/about-mental-illness/mental-health-by-the-numbers/.

105 Mental Health America. "The State of Mental Health in America," n.d. https://www.mhanational.org/issues/state-mental-health-america.

106 Wehrwein, Peter. "Astounding Increase in Antidepressant Use by Americans." Harvard Health, October 20, 2011. https://www.health.harvard.edu/blog/astounding-increase-in-antidepressant-use-by-americans-201110203624.

107 "Physical Activity Improves Mood for People Serious Mental Illness." 2009. ScienceDaily. January 9, 2009. https://www.sciencedaily.com/releases/2009/01/090114110931.htm

108 Stephens, Thomas. "Physical Activity and Mental Health in the United States and Canada: Evidence From Four Population Surveys." Preventive Medicine 17, no. 1 (January 1, 1988): 35–47. https://doi.org/10.1016/0091-7435(88)90070-9.

109 Gerber, Markus, Serge Brand, Christian Herrmann, Flora Colledge, Edith Holsboer-Trachsler, and Uwe Pühse. "Increased Objectively Assessed Vigorous-intensity Exercise Is Associated With Reduced Stress, Increased Mental Health and Good Objective and Subjective Sleep in Young Adults." Physiology & Behavior 135 (June 4, 2014): 17–24. https://doi.org/10.1016/j.physbeh.2014.05.047.

110 Ratey, John J., MD. 2019. "Can Exercise Help Treat Anxiety?" Harvard Health. October 24, 2019. https://www.health.harvard.edu/blog/can-exercise-help-treat-anxiety-2019102418096

111 Pixar Animation Studios. "WALL-E — Pixar Animation Studios," n.d. https://www.pixar.com/wall-e.

112 Mayo Clinic. "How Much Exercise Do You Really Need?," n.d. https://www.mayoclinic.org/healthy-lifestyle/fitness/expert-answers/exercise/faq-20057916.

113 O'Neil, Adrienne, Shae E. Quirk, Siobhan Housden, Sharon L. Brennan, Lana J. Williams, Julie A. Pasco, Michael Berk, and Felice N. Jacka. "Relationship Between Diet and Mental Health in Children and Adolescents: A Systematic Review." American Journal of Public Health 104, no. 10 (October 1, 2014): e31–42. https://doi.org/10.2105/ajph.2014.302110.

114 HealthyChildren.org. "Food Additives: What Parents Should Know," n.d. https://www.healthychildren.org/English/healthy-living/nutrition/Pages/Food-Additives.aspx.

115 Graham, James. 2016. "Nutrition and Health in Children and the Role of the Healthcare Worker." Ausmed Education Pty Ltd. November 1, 2016. https://www.ausmed.com/cpd/articles/nutrition for-children.

116 "Physical Activity Facts | CDC Archive," n.d. https://archive.cdc.gov/#/details?url=https://www.cdc.gov/healthyschools/physicalactivity/facts.htm.

117 Bruijns, Brianne A., Stephanie Truelove, Andrew M. Johnson, Jason Gilliland, and Patricia Tucker. 2020. "Infants' and Toddlers' Physical Activity and Sedentary Time as Measured by Accelerometry: A Systematic Review and Meta-analysis." International Journal of Behavioral Nutrition and Physical Activity 17 (1). https://doi.org/10.1186/s12966-020-0912-4.

118 Russek, Linda G., and Gary E. Schwartz. 1997. "Feelings of Parental Caring Predict Health Status in Midlife: A 35-year Follow-up of the Harvard Mastery of Stress Study." Journal of Behavioral Medicine 20 (1): 1–13. https://doi.org/10.1023/a:1025525428213.

119 PubMed. "Narrative Descriptions of Parental Love and Caring Predict Health Status in Midlife: A 35-year Follow-up of the Harvard Mastery of Stress Study," November 1, 1996. https://pubmed.ncbi.nlm.nih.gov/8942044/.

ACKNOWLEDGEMENTS

We are deeply grateful to the individuals who contributed to How to Soul in countless ways—through their wisdom, encouragement, and unwavering support.

A heartfelt thank you to Nancy Spielberg, Peter Himmelman, Rabbi Yitzchak Breitowitz, Bishop Robert Sterns, Lori Palatnik, Dr. Michael Oren, Leon VanderPol, Brock Mealer, Madelana Ferrara, and Dr. Jennifer Simmons for taking the time to review the book and share their thoughtful endorsements.

To our beta readers—Evonne Marzouk, David Comins, Cindy Nehrbass, and Heidi Schneider—your insights and feedback helped refine this book into what it is today.

We are grateful to our publisher, Dr. Yael Maoz, of Beverly House Press and Emuna Press, for her expertise, guidance, patience, and unwavering support throughout this journey.

A special thank you to our developmental editor, Kate Hopper, whose insights and belief in How to Soul from its inception were invaluable.

We extend our appreciation to our book sponsors, Dean Lambert and David Sergi, whose generosity made this project possible.

To Raphael Shore, for introducing us to our publisher and for sharing his wisdom along the way—thank you for your guidance and support.

ATARA'S GRATITUDE

To my incredible children, Baila, Yaakov, and Yaeli—thank you for your love and patience as I balanced a full-time job, writing this book, and being your mom. I am endlessly blessed to be the mother of three such beautiful and loving souls. Thank you to my son-in-law, Moshe Farkash, for his love, support and excitement about this book.

To Chaya Esther (Hilary) Presberg, Rikki Holtzman, and Lesley Schofield—your endless support and boundless love mean the world to me. May you always be blessed with goodness.

To my parents, Dr. Robert and Joye Sigelman, for a lifetime of love and support through every age, stage, crisis, and celebration—thank you for being my foundation.

And above all, to God, for the opportunity to be a vessel for bringing Divine light into the world in this way. May this endeavor be blessed for the good.

DOV'S GRATITUDE

I must begin by thanking God, who created my body and soul and fused them together for a life filled with challenges, enjoyment, and meaning.

To my wife, Hadas, and my children and grandchildren - your existence and love is my greatest blessing.

To Dr. Allen and Leah Lipman Zeiger - for your unwavering support. To my father, Judge Ronald Lipman, of blessed memory - for his continuous inspiration.

And to my teachers, who have taught and motivated me to live a soul-focused life - thank you for guiding me on this journey.

ABOUT ATARA WEISBERGER

Atara Weisberger is a National Board Certified Health & Wellness Coach and Certified Deep Transformational Coach with over 20 years of expertise in integrative healing. As the founder of The Tribe, a holistic wellness community, she merges spiritual growth with modern self-care, empowering individuals to embrace their inner wisdom and live with purpose.

Atara's career began in environmental policy, working with the U.S. EPA and environmental nonprofits before transitioning to health and wellness. She has developed transformative programs for cancer survivors, co-founded The Tribe Athletics and Fitness, and has been featured in *Nashim Magazine*, *Jew in the City*, and *Times of Israel*.

Her journey from a secular upbringing to a more observant Jewish life fuels her mission to help others find meaning and connection in today's fast-paced world. Through her coaching, writing, and workshops, she guides people toward deeper self-awareness, balance, and joy.

Connect with Atara and download your free heart meditations at

https://HowToSoulBook.com/

HOW TO SOUL

ABOUT RABBI DOV LIPMAN

Rabbi Dov Lipman is an educator, speaker, and author dedicated to bridging faith, education, and public service. A former member of Israel's 19th Knesset—the first American-born MK in 30 years—he holds rabbinic ordination from Ner Israel Rabbinical College and a master's in education from Johns Hopkins University.

With over 20 years of experience teaching students at all levels, Rabbi Lipman is a sought-after speaker on topics related to Israel and Jewish faith. He is the author of ten books on Judaism and Israel and has been featured in CNN, Fox News, The New York Times, BBC, ABC Australia, and The Ben Shapiro Show.

As the founder of Yad L'Olim, an organization assisting new immigrants to Israel, Rabbi Lipman continues his mission of advocacy and leadership. He lives in Israel with his wife, Hadas, their four children, and five grandchildren.

Connect with Rabbi Lipman and explore his work at

https://RabbiDovLipman.com/